Hot dog People

and other bite-size Sacrifices

THE ADVENTURES OF RAISING THREE BOYS
WRITTEN & ILLUSTRATED BY DAN MAGDICH

Hot dog People
and other bite-size sacrifices

Written, Illustrated and Designed by Dan Magdich

Edited by Alaina Sapienza

Title Typography by Paxton and Colton Magdich

Additional Artwork by Paxton, Colton and Greyson Magdich

Cover and "I HATE KETCHUP" Font Photography by David Kelly

Family Photography by Frank Vilsack

Lived by The Best Mom and Wife in the World Crystal Lyn O'Brien Magdich

Animal Media Group books may be ordered through
Consortium Book Sales and Distribution Company or contacting:

ANIMAL MEDIA GROUP
100 First Avenue, Suite 1100, Pittsburgh, PA 15222
animalmediagroup.com
412-566-5656

FIRST EDITION SEPTEMBER 2019
ISBN: 978-1-947895-08-9
e-book: 978-1-947895-16-4

This book is dedicated to Gavin Max

and his three brothers Paxton, Colton and Greyson.

And to Crystal for her selfless

and tireless efforts day in and day out.

Love,

Dad

Someone once told me
"DAN. You should really write
these stories down." and I said
"you know I **NEVER** thought of that."
- quote by the author

Despite the colorful illustrations and smiling hot dog on the cover this is not a children's book. This book, however, is about kids. Specifically my three boys (Paxton, 7, Colton, 5, and Greyson, 3), their imaginative personalities and off the wall takes on life.

The stories in this book are true and depict the heartfelt chaos of kids that every parent can relate to. The honest and conversational writing serves as a reminder that your toddler isn't the first to yell "son of a bitch!" in Target and they certainly won't be the last.

Put the kids to bed, pour yourself a drink, and enjoy.

- Dan

2015

chapter

I

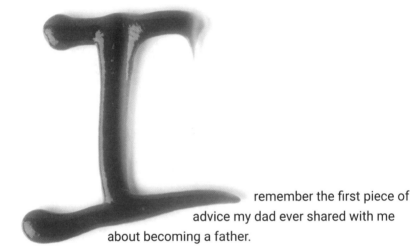 remember the first piece of advice my dad ever shared with me about becoming a father.

"When you have kids, you won't find this funny anymore."

He was short of breath, buckled over on one knee and slowly recovering from a nut shot, courtesy of me and my tiny child fists. Or maybe it was my tiny child feet. Maybe both, I can't remember since it was twenty-five years ago.

But I do remember the look of pain on his face. That look was hilarious. All red with anguish like an overripe tomato, beads of sweat dancing along his furrowed brow. His face was so wrinkled up and contorted that his moustache was practically touching his chin. Oh boy! My favorite look! It always made me laugh until I was on the verge of pissing my pants.

I didn't realize it at the time but that look paired with Dad's ten words were meaningful. His slow, thought-provoking delivery of each syllable always stuck with me and I never realized why until years later.

At the time I thought he was only talking like that because I knocked the wind out of him. Looking back I'm sure that was half of it. I remember laughing that innocently annoying childhood laugh before skipping away like a little shithead. I probably shouted "GOTCHA!" because I got him. I got him real good. But truthfully, Dad was the one who got me in the long run.

One evening in August 2015 I called my dad. It was late, around 10:30 at night.

My mom answered the phone.

"Hey...is everything ok?" she asked, in that soft, should-I-be-worried voice that all veteran moms have mastered.

She had good reason to bring it out. A call out of the blue at this ungodly hour?! Someone must be dead, dying or on fire.

ME: Oh yeah, sorry, everything's fine.
I just need to talk to Dad for a second.

MOM: Ok, he just dozed off on the couch.
Want me to wake him up?

ME: Yeah...I mean It's not an emergency but
I'd like to talk to him.

MOM: Ok...

A muffled dialogue is exchanged.

DAD: Hello?

ME: Hey! Sorry to wake you up and call so late but there's something I really need to tell you.

DAD: Ooooook?

ME: I'm sorry.

DAD: Sorry? For what?

ME: For all the intentional or accidental nut shots I gave you as I was growing up. I no longer find this funny and you were right. I'd understand when I had kids.

The line went silent.

Crap. He's pissed. I woke him up for this. He's probably thinking, Wow! Your kids punched you in the bean bag. Big deal. Grow a pair. Damn kids. Even as adults they gotta pester you over the stupidest shit.

His silence was broken by a fit of laughter. But not just any laughter—a familiar innocent, annoying, childlike laughter. The kind of laughter that complacency buries for twenty-five years.

I deserved this. He deserved this. I let him have those uninterrupted moments of reflection because he earned them.

Dad's laughter subsided and was followed by a short "Thank you," and "I told you so," and finally, "I love you. Good night."

At this point in time we (my wife, Crystal, and I) had two sons, Paxton and Colton. Those dudes were at the perfect height for sack tapping. Everything led to a bump. Hugs became headbutts, wild elbows greeted me like handshakes. Nutshots became so commonplace that I ended up in the ER with some sort of ball infection.

Who woulda thunk it? I didn't even know that was possible. Apparently it is. And it's caused by "trauma." The kind of trauma a speed bag endures.

Somehow my two (at the time) awesome and adorable kids punched, kicked, flicked, elbowed, kneed and everything else awful'd me in the testicles so many times that they got fucking infected.

Good Lord, the pain. Jesus help me, the pain. It *sucked*.

I mean, ball pain always sucks. But this pain was on another level of suck. Just thinking about it gives me this weird pinching turtle-retreating-into-its-shell sensation. It was a sort of sharp stabbing thing, but with an internal infernal tugging pull.

Fucking turtles, man. I still can't look at them the same. They remind me of the pinch. Oy vey, now I'm sweating and my knees are weak. Is this PTSD?

At the time I thought it was kidney stones, but like, in my balls which didn't make sense but Google and WebMD had me sold on kidney stones. It was either that or something far far worse that would cause my coin purse to turn purple and balloon up like an eggplant.

I was gunning for kidney stones.

Thankfully, it wasn't kidney stones or that horrible eggplant thing. It was something much more hilarious. Despite the horrific pain, I couldn't help but find my predicament incredibly funny. The whole scene was so bizarre.

Picture me lying in a hospital bed as doctor after doctor examined my diddly bits, with a never-ending barrage of does-this-hurts and what-about-nows. My answer was always affirmative but what followed or preceded was a variety of expletives, a fit of crying laughter, or a resounding "JESUS" followed by a kitten-like whimper.

To date, that was the one and only time I've had morphine. So either I'm a huge baby or my balls really did hurt that bad.

It was only fitting that my dad was there with me. He and I were in the midst of one of many DIY projects at my house when I dropped to the floor, screaming about the sudden and intense pain in my balls.

Paxton and Colton thought that look was hilarious! My face all red with anguish like an overripe tomato. Beads of sweat dancing along my furrowed brow. My sons began imitating my cries as they also fell to the floor grasping their boyhood.

OH HI KARMA! SO NICE OF YOU TO SHOW UP. BETTER LATE THAN NEVER. DRINKS ARE IN THE BACK. PLEASE HELP YOURSELF. I'M A BIT PREOCCUPIED WITH THIS SEARING PAIN IN MY SCROTUM.

Fast forward ninety minutes, and I'm in the ER on the receiving end of an incredibly awkward ultrasound. Turns out those things aren't just for babies. They can be used to see all sorts of things. Like infections. In my balls.

I left the ER with a prescription for painkillers and an antibiotic called owmyscroteicillin or something. I don't remember the real name. After three days the infection mostly cleared up, and I could walk again. But karma wasn't done with me yet.

We decided to go to our all time favorite store, Target. It felt like the perfect place to re-enter society and buy a bunch of stuff we didn't really need but would inevitably purchase because, Target.

As I pushed the cart with the boys in it, I saw someone who looked strangely familiar.

She and I exchanged glances, and I could tell she recognized me from somewhere. I asked Crystal if the lady looked familiar to her. Nope. Not at all.

Hmm. That's weird.

I knew I knew her from somewhere. High school? College maybe?

"Excuse me, you look—"

It dawned on me who she was before I could finish the sentence.

I would have got the fuck outta dodge faster but I was still sore. Speed wasn't really an option. Instead I clumsily pulled the kid-filled cart in reverse, bumping into shelves lined with discounted toilet paper.

Crystal looked at me like I was molting my exoskeleton.

"What are you doing?" she asked through her teeth.

I leaned in close to her so the boys wouldn't hear. "That's the nurse who scanned my *stuff*."

Apparently, it wasn't close enough.

PAXTON: Dad! That lady scanned your weiner?! OH MY GOD! Mom did you hear that?

He stands up in the cart and points to the unsuspecting health professional standing across the aisle.

PAXTON: That lady scanned Dad's weiner!

COLTON: Ha ha! PEE PEE!

The poor woman was staring at us, because how could she not? I didn't know what else to do so I said hi to her like a big dumb fucking idiot. Naturally, she got weirded out and quickly walked away. I could feel my face reddening darker than the crimson cart carrying my sons.

Things were back to normal a couple of weeks later. The pain was gone. It was still embarrassing to think of what happened in Target but, whatever. I'd *probably* never have to see that ultrasound nurse again.

The kids were just happy I could wrestle again. I was happy I could wrestle again. All was right in the world.

Right in the middle of my glorious return to the ring, BAM! The foot of an overexcited toddler came crashing down from the top rope.

"Dammit," I winced.

I composed myself, sat up and bestowed upon them the same dadly wisdom my dad bestowed upon me.

"When you have kids, you won't find this funny anymore."

The boys didn't care. They laughed and skipped away, just like I did when I was a little shithead.

But those words stuck with me and hopefully, they'll stick with them. Even if it takes them two decades and a set of tender testes to realize their importance.

NOT MOM

"Mom makes breakfast first."

"Mom gives me the yellow cup."

"That's not what Mom does."

♡ A HAIKU FROM HUSBAND TO WIFE ♡

The many looks of kids' wear

The "Mom Dressed Me" Look

The "Dad Dressed Me" Look

The "DIY Superhero" Look

The "WTF Are You Wearing?" Look

The "I Dressed Myself" Look

The "I Dressed Myself And Put A Shirt On" Look

The "Billy Madison" Look

The "I'm In Kindergarten And Brand Names Already Matter" Look

2016

chapter

2

Crystal and I constantly ask our boys questions about life, their ambitions and their interests. Sometimes we do this to get them thinking. Other times it's for our own amusement. But every time we ask those questions we all learn something, and it's taught us that talking with your kids is one of the most important things a parent can do.

Our boys' answers can vary from cute to terrifying to wise beyond their years. The conversation known as The Cheese Hustle was equals parts of all three.

One Mother's Day, Paxton and Colton really wanted to take Mom to Fat Head's (a local Pittsburgh restaurant) for lunch. It's pretty much their favorite restaurant of all time, so much that Colton asks for Fat Head's gift cards for Christmas.

I'm always happy to go to Fat Head's because they have a killer beer selection and sandwiches the size of your head. Crystal loves their pepperoni rolls. We both love that the boys clean their plates every time we visit.

Driving home after lunch.

COLTON: Hey Daaaaad?

ME: Yeah buddy?

COLTON: I wanna tell you something.

ME: What's up?

"WHEN I GROW UP I'M GONNA BE SUPER RICH!"

ME: Rich? REALLY?

COLTON: YEAH! Super RICH!

ME: Super rich? And how are you going to make all your money?

COLTON: Well...I'm gonna...

I can see his mind searching for the most logical answer.

COLTON: I'm gonna hustle that cheese.

ME: Hustle cheese?

COLTON: Yeah man. I'm gonna hustle cheese. I'm gonna make that cheese, play that cheese, roll that cheese, push that cheese, sell that cheese. You know. I'm gonna hustle cheese. All day. Every day.

ME: Ok, but how is hustling cheese going to make you lots of money?

COLTON: Dad!

Colton facepalms himself.

COLTON: PYRAMID SCHEME.

ME: A pyramid scheme?

Crystal and I exchange WTF glances.

ME: How do you know what a pyramid scheme is?

COLTON: Dad, come on, I know everything.

ME: Ok, go on. How's this "Cheese Hustle" work?

COLTON: See I got this "cheese" (he actually used air quotes). It's "good cheese" (air quotes again). I'm up here talkin' cheese and get people who want the cheese. I tell them I got the best cheese so they start hustling the cheese for me. Then I take their money and they don't get cheese.

He stumped me. I have no response. I sit quietly and try to process how my three-year-old knows what a pyramid scheme is.

After approximately seven minutes of complete silence I decide to shift the dialogue back to a normal conversation.

ME: Dudes. Thank you for taking Mommy to lunch with me.

PAXTON: You're welcome.

COLTON: YEAH! It was pretty fan-tas-tic!

ME: What was your favorite part?

PAXTON: The big Fat Head's guy logo on the door!

COLTON: I LIKED EVERYTHING! CAN WE COME BACK AGAIN?!

ME: Yes, of course.

COLTON: OH! I liked when we saw the Fat Head's logo guy in the bathroom and I told him his head was SO FAT.

ME: Colton, I told you that wasn't the guy from the logo. That was just a guy with a fat head. I don't think he appreciated you telling

ME (cont.): him his head was so fat. We need to talk about bathroom etiquette, boys.

PAXTON: Eddy what the what?

ME: Etiquette. It's the rules. Like rule number one in the men's room—don't talk to anyone.

COLTON: Why?

ME: It's uncomfortable.

PAXTON: What's rule number two?

ME: Never compliment a man's watch at the urinal.

2017

chapter

3

efore we even had kids, Crystal and I agreed that we would lead our family by example. We've always believed the best way to instill strong ethics, manners, values and confidence in our children is to live those things every day and share them as a family.

Community is a big thing in our home. We believe that family extends beyond the five of us, our bulldog (Penelope), grandparents, cousins, aunts and uncles, etc. Family includes neighbors. Our city. Local charities and businesses. We teach our boys that family is community, and it's important to support and give back because family should be there for each other.

We make it a point to show the boys that kindness is welcome in any form, at any time of the year. This means toy drives, food banks, random acts of kindness and so on. It's nice to watch the boys learn how rewarding it can be to do good for others.

An easy way of showing support for the community around here is by attending fish frys. It's a simple concept—a church or volunteer fire department fries up a whole lot of fish, you bring your family and enjoy, knowing the price of your meal is going to a good cause.

Kids don't pay attention. Ever. I shouldn't say ever. They do pay attention when it's something they care about like construction trucks or Pokémon. But fish frys? That's boring. So when the topic of visiting one came up, Paxton was confused and curious and wanted to know more.

Even though he'd been to a number of them.

Crystal and I are talking about hitting up a fish fry.

PAXTON: Dad?

ME: Dude?

"WHAT THE HECK IS A FISH FRY?"

ME: It's like a cookout but it's indoors. And instead of burgers and hot dogs they serve fish, shrimp, mac and cheese, colesl—

PAXTON: That sounds boring. What do you eat at a fish fry?

ME: Fish.

PAXTON: Yeah yeah, I know that. But like what do me and Colton eat there?

ME: They have fish sticks for you guys. Plus there's mac and cheese.

PAXTON: Gooey mac and cheese or the blue kind?

Gooey mac and cheese is Velveeta shells and cheese. Blue kind is Kraft.

COLTON: I LOVE GOOEY mac and cheese!

ME: I'm not sure. Each fish fry has a different mac and cheese. Sometimes it's the blue kind, sometimes it's gooey and

ME (cont.): sometimes it's homemade. That's my favorite mac and cheese.

PAXTON: I don't like how that sounds. What else can I eat if they don't have blue mac?

ME: Fish sticks.

I can see a puzzled look overcoming his face as he is processing some sort of thought.

PAXTON: ...ahhh

COLTON: FISH STICKS?!

PAXTON: I don't think I want to eat those.

ME: Dudes. You'll love them. Trust me.

PAXTON: I don't know about that. That just sounds...so...weird and so gross.

ME: Weird and gross? What's weird and gross about fish sticks?

PAXTON: Like, why would I eat those?

ME: Because they're like a chicken nugget but with fish instead of chicken.

PAXTON: No they're not. They're fish sticks. They sound disgusting.

ME: Just try them when we get there and if you don't like it then you can eat mac and cheese.

PAXTON: Dad! There is no way that I'm putting FISH WEINERS in mouth. I'm not gonna eat any FISH WEINERS, ever.

COLTON: DAD! I'LL EAT A FISH WEINER!!

Now I have the puzzled look on my face. How'd we get to weiners from fish sticks?

ME: Uhhh...no guys, they're not fish weiners. They are fish STICKS. STICKS with an S. Not DICKS with a D.

PAXTON: Oh. Well that makes sense.

COLTON: I'll still eat a fish weiner.

ME: Let's just order pizza.

So, can anyone help get these two an internship with Trey Parker and Matt Stone? I have a feeling they'd be a great fit.

Download Google translate.

A child will inevitably change the default language on a device to something like Korean or Swahili and the app's camera feature will be your BFF.

Dan's DADVICE

2016

chapter

4

Kids love to play pretend, Crystal and I find it's best to let their minds wander. We encourage the creation of worlds, scenarios, obstacles, encounters, and adventures in our boys' heads. It helps to stoke their creativity, and honestly it keeps them distracted for short, sweet, merciful chunks of time.

Free babysitting aside, we encourage our kids to be imaginative and resourceful because as we grow up that instinctual creativity fades. We begin to accept reality for what it is and priorities shift from battling monsters to more "age appropriate" activities like mortgages and investment portfolios. It's a bummer.

I hope our sons' creativity plays an integral role in their adult lives. Maybe they'll be screenwriters or artists or those living statues in New Orleans. Anything but a cog in the machine. Or a serial killer.

Though serial killers can be pretty creative.

All three of our boys have their own outlets. Each outlet impacts the dynamic of our home. There are days when all three boys enjoy one another's outlet as they lovingly play together and share. It's harmonious as hell. Then there are days when their outlets piss each other off and incite riots.

Paxton loves to draw and build forts. He's the (first) Lego kid of the house and is fascinated by the details in everything. He loves figuring out how things work. He also loves making loud noises. His favorite noise to make is "eeeEEEHHHHHH."

Greyson is the youngest, ten months old at the time of this particular incident. G is a mischief-maker and a master of the eye roll. He's a busy little dude who finds creative ways to mess shit up. Nothing is off-limits and his older brothers think he's hilarious—especially when he runs around the house screaming for no apparent reason, a mile-long trail of toilet paper clutched in his hands.

His older brothers were nowhere near this active as toddlers so Crystal and I can only speculate on how his mischievous nature will evolve as he grows up.

Colton has approximately eighty-two personalities that he cycles through at any given moment and God forbid we don't realize the second he transforms from Colton to Captain America Colton or Hulk Colton or Catboy Colton or Leonardo Colton or just plain Ninja Colton.

Then there's Just Colton, who is Colton but with a hat on. Just Colton is like the cocoon of all his personas and only Colton knows which butterfly will break free. I can't forget Bad Guy Colton. Bad Guy Colton is similar to Just Colton but he sports a backwards hat and clenched fists.

The differences are minor but knowing them will help you avoid the hellfire that reigns down should you inadvertently call him by the wrong name.

I don't always know what game the boys are playing, or which Colton is running around the living room at any given time. And most of the time I'm pretty sure the boys don't either. They make up rules as they go.

Paxton is the oldest and likes to be the leader. He expects his younger brothers to fall in line. That worked for a while until Colton realized he's his own person and can do what he wants at his own pace. And Greyson, well, he's an anarchist so fuck the rules here's a brick through your window.

On the day of the Password Incident, the older two boys were running around the house as usual. The game *was* hide-and-seek before Colton emerged from a hiding spot as Thor Colton. His costume was new and also three sizes too big. Amazon shipped us the wrong size but Colton's excitement level was at an eleven for his Thor costume so we kept it and just rolled up the sleeves and legs. He'll grow into it.

Keep in mind that Colton doesn't tell anyone when he transforms into an alternate persona, it just happens. Paxton missed the switch and attempted to squeeze by Colton so he could hide and Colton could count.

The problem? Paxton said "Excuse me, Colton," when he should have said "Excuse me, *Thor* Colton."

Thor Colton immediately blocked the hallway with his hammer and shouted in a very deep Thor voice—

"WHAT'S THE PASSWORD?!"

The brothers lock eyes. Paxton scratches his chin and taps his foot.

PAXTON: The password is...

Thor Colton's breathing intensifies. He white-knuckles his hammer and stares down his brother as if his eyes were shouting SAY THE WRONG THING AND YOU WILL FOREVER BE BANISHED FROM ASGARD, LOKI!

PAXTON: ...suck my butthole.

THOR COLTON: THAT IS CORRECT. YOU MAY PASS.

I'm dumbfounded.

I'm amused.

I'm wondering if that was actually the password.

Was it a lucky guess or just humorous enough to warrant entry?

Or was Paxton telling his younger brother to piss off?

ME: Woah. Woah. Woah. What's that password?!

THE BOYS IN UNISON: SUCK MY BUTTHOLE!

ME: No. Not anymore. Pick a new password. "Suck my butthole" cannot be the password.

PAXTON: Why?

THOR COLTON: DAD! SUCK MY BUTTHOLE IS THE BEST PASSWORD. NO BAD GUYS WILL EVER GUESS IT AND GET IN THE HOUSE!

Oh my God, he's still using his deep Thor voice.

ME: "Suck my butthole" is an incredibly rude thing to say. It's not something nice boys should say to anyone, including each other. I don't wanna explain the finer details of what that password means so let's just leave it at that. Please pick a new password.

THE BOYS IN UNISON: Ok, Dad. Sorry.

ME: It's ok. Thank you.

THOR COLTON: PAXTON, WE NEED A NEW PASSWORD!

PAXTON: I know. I know. Lemme think.

THOR COLTON: WHAT ABOUT BUTTHOLE. JUST BUTTHOLE?

PAXTON: No. That's too similar.

THOR COLTON: OK. WHAT ABOUT...

THE BOYS IN UNISON: SUCK MY WEINER!

ME: NOPE. NO. NO. NO. NOT THAT. Go back to "suck my butthole." I'd rather "suck my butthole" be the password. Or just "butthole." Yeah, just "butthole." Only "butthole." No sucking of anything for a password. The password can not include "suck" or "my."

THE BOYS IN UNISON: What about booger?

ME: BOOGER! Perfect password. Yes. Use that, please.

The dynamic duo vanish down the hallway to their room and continue playing.

I gotta admit those were some top-notch passwords. No bad guy would guess those. Our home was safe...for now.

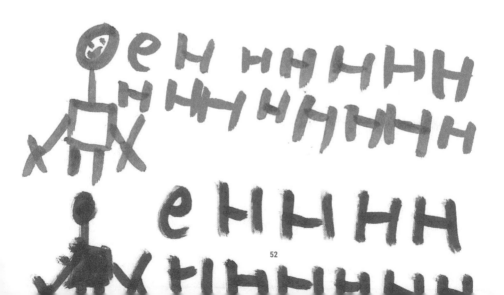

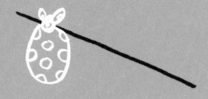

How do you do it?
These boys are freaking psycho.
Don't run away, please.

♡ A HAIKU FROM HUSBAND TO WIFE ♡

Booty shaking hips.
Seriously, why and how?
Our boys sure can twerk!

♡ A HAIKU FROM HUSBAND TO WIFE ♡

Play it Off!

Toddlers babble incoherent gibberish but will use "shit" in the correct context because they heard you use it in the correct context.

Dan's DADVICE

Colors
according to
GREYSON

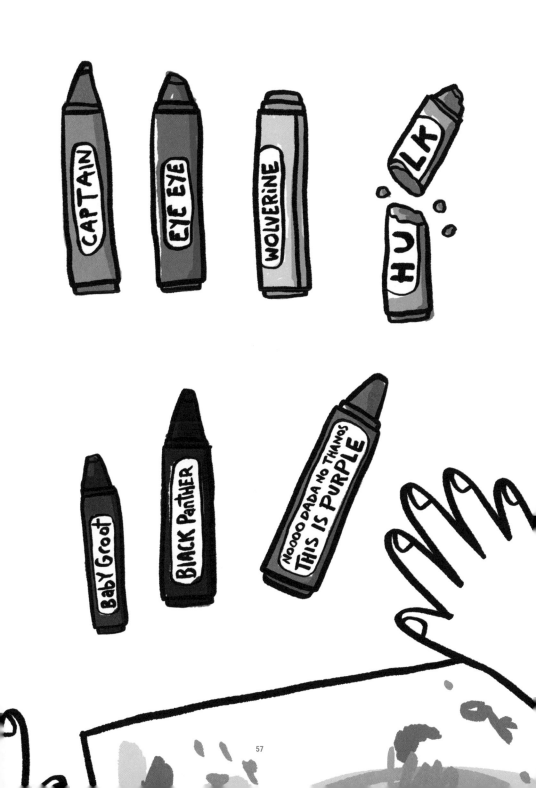

2014

chapter
5

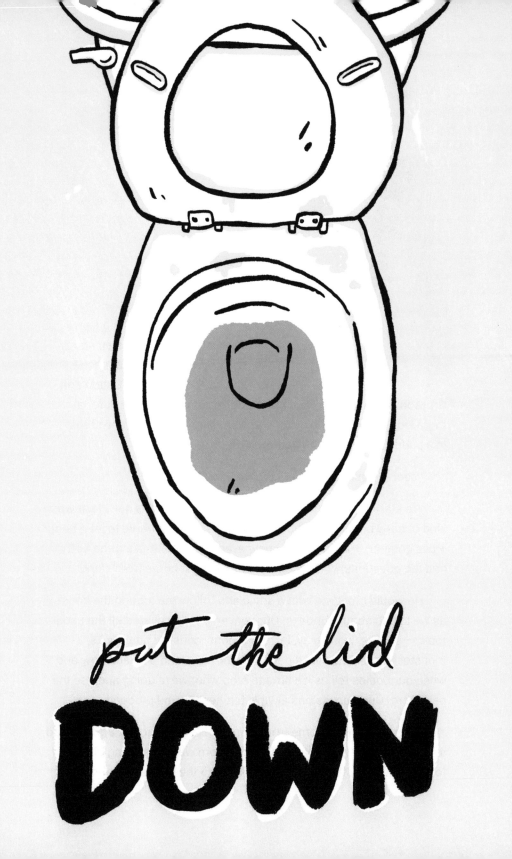

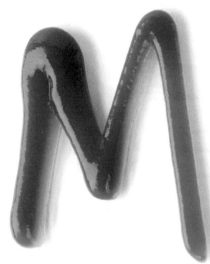y poor wife. Three boys *and* a husband. Eek. Crystal is a saint, seriously. She's our Queen and she knows it, or at least I hope she knows it. Paxton, Colton and Greyson could not ask for a better Mom and I could not ask for a more kick-ass wife. She never stops smiling, even when she steps in a puddle of piss on the bathroom floor.

I secretly think that's her favorite thing to step in.

We started potty training Paxton around two and a half. That was kind of early but he was showing an interest in the whole toilet + poop + pee concept. He wanted to know everything about using the potty, and the questions would start as soon as I got home from work.

He would greet me with a smile and follow me around the house as we talked about our days. Our conversations covered all the usual topics—snacks, work, play, farts, cartoons, construction trucks, monster trucks. Then we'd get to toilets, poop and pee, and how and when our bodies tell us it's time to stop what we're doing and use the bathroom. Our discussions always felt healthy and productive.

One day I arrived home from work really having to go. Bad. So bad it hurt. Not like *it* hurt but the pressure from waiting so long did. I had to go so bad that the moment I walked into the house I immediately shuffled to the bathroom, barely able to stand up straight. I silently cursed myself for drinking so much water before my thirty-minute commute home from the office.

Paxton followed me into the bathroom and stood directly behind me as I went. My insides were constricting too much to consider why letting my two-and-a-half-year-old stand out of view while I was pretty helpless might be a bad idea.

It started out harmless enough. Paxton asked why I was walking funny and if that meant I had to go pee. As I started to explain the what and the why to him, I realized he was being incredibly quiet. Too quiet for a kid with a thousand questions about bathroom habits.

I glanced over my right shoulder and realized he wasn't standing behind me anymore. A giggle came from my left side.

My head snapped around. I looked over and down to find Paxton with his hands on the toilet seat, laughing at me. I knew what he was about to do but couldn't react fast enough.

"DON'T FORGET TO PUT THE LID DOWN!" he shouted, slamming it closed.

I panicked. I couldn't stop. The urge to pee was too strong, and when it's that bad it's impossible to kink the hose. I began peeing over the closed toilet.

I yelled for help but all that came out was a pathetic squeak that only made Paxton laugh harder. I held him to one location with my free hand as I frantically looked around the bathroom.

I couldn't make it to the shower. Pax was in the way. I looked at the trash can. Paxton followed my eyeline and darted to block that solution.

The sink! I shuffled over to the sink and emptied what was left of my still-screaming bladder. Perfect. Disaster avoided! That could have been messy!

I looked around the room and realized my eyes guided my stream around like the world's shittiest service dog. Pee soaked everything. The toilet, walls, floor, trash can, shower curtain, vanity. Everything. Except Paxton.

At least there was that.

Right about then is when Crystal walked into the bathroom. She looked at me peeing in the sink, and then the purple-with-laughter-Paxton at my side.

Her eyes went back to me. Then to the toilet. The floor. The shower curtain. She looked at me again.

And...she smiled.

"At least you kept him dry," she said. "I'll grab the Clorox and some towels."

Potty Training boYs?

Start outside.
Trees are bigger and easier to hit than a toilet.

Dan's DADVICE

2014

chapter

6

I don't recall how old I was when my parents labeled me "officially potty trained." And honestly, I'm not sure that I am entirely potty trained even as an adult. Every kid learns at a different age and at different speeds, even into their thirties.

Potty training Paxton was a process. But isn't that the case with every kid? Pax acts and talks a lot older than he really is. He's the two going on twenty type and when he wants to do something he puts his mind and every ounce of his being into it. Conversely, when he's over something it's over.

Not long after the oh-so-hilarious Put The Lid Down incident, Pax decided he was ready. He asked us if he could start peeing and pooping like a big boy. And we figured, why not? He wanted to do it.

We quickly worked out a bulletproof system: M&M's! M&M's were his crutch. The kid would do anything for an M&M. Hell, his face would light up like a Christmas tree when he'd reach the letter M in the alphabet.

It was brilliant. Go pee on the toilet, get M&M's. Go poop, get a star. If he got five stars, that would earn him a trip to the toy section at

Target to pick out a diecast Hot Wheels Monster Truck. Paxton picked the system up quick and we figured he was going to be potty trained in no time.

Then he started to find loopholes.

He first attempted to barter with Pap-Pap. The proposition? If Pap peed on the toilet and said it was Paxton, he'd get a bigger haul of M&M's and the two of them would split the take. It'd be their secret.

Pap didn't agree to the terms, so Paxton went another route.

He figured if he only peed part of the pee and held the rest for later, he could rake in more candy-coated chocolates over the course of multiple trips to the bathroom. Yup, little dude started to conserve his urine so he could get more M&M's.

Crystal and I caught onto that almost immediately. It's pretty tricky explaining to a two-and-a-half-year-old what a UTI or bladder infection is, so I improvised and told him that if he held it too long his head would fall off. And just like that we were back to normal peeing.

Until cold and flu season hit.

The wheels fell off the wagon. Our house got hit with a bug. Poop, puke, and pee galore.

Poor Paxton, he reverted back to diapers. And not by choice. The kid couldn't make it to the bathroom in time and his little body wasn't giving him enough warning when the literal shit was going to hit the figurative fan.

After two days he was back to normal. No barf. No explosive diarrhea. Order restored. Time to get back to potty training.

Only there was one problem.

PAXTON: You know, Mom and Dad? I like diapers. They're easy.

CRYSTAL: Buddy, you were doing so good. You can't go back to diapers.

PAXTON: But what if I poop my pants again?

CRYSTAL: That's called an accident. Your dad has them all the time. It's ok. If you have an accident, I'll help you.

PAXTON: Can I think about it?

ME: Sure.

Later that afternoon.

PAXTON: I gotta pee.

From that moment forward he used the potty. But only to pee. Pooping wasn't happening. The diarrhea ruined him. He had a real fear of not making it to the potty, and that fear manifested into some sort of twisted irrational toddler logic—If I'm going to poop my pants then I might as well do it in a diaper.

The poop battle continued for some time. New monster truck toys weren't enough for Paxton to overcome his diarrhea anxieties. Negotiations began. Both sides sat down and talked things over. We reached a compromise: If Paxton pooped and peed on the potty for an entire week, Sunday to Saturday, then he could get a skateboard. We shook on it.

Fast forward seven days. We're at Toys 'R Us and Pax was proudly deciding between a Spider-Man or Teenage Mutant Ninja Turtles skateboard. He went with Spider-Man. Solid choice, dude.

Everyone was stoked. Paxton mastered pooping! He and I spent that Saturday afternoon skateboarding up and down the hallway. He got the balance thing down pretty fast and built up enough confidence to "pop wheelies." I tried explaining to him that those were called manuals and not wheelies, but he insisted he knew what was what and asked me to stop calling it "a manual." Whatever you say, poser.

By Sunday night he was riding his Spider-Man skateboard up and down the hall all by himself. He even slept with it nestled under his arm.

Paxton was so proud of himself. And Crystal and I were equally proud of him.

That following Monday afternoon, Crystal walked to the end of the driveway to grab the mail. As she entered the garage she heard Paxton (above) skateboarding up and down the hallway as baby Colton jumped in his crib, laughing and yelling at his brother.

Then the house went quiet. Typically when that happened the boys were doing something mischievous together, or Paxton had climbed into Colton's crib to "read" stories to him. The latter is adorable and heartwarming, but that day it was not the latter.

Crystal heard Paxton running. Up the hall. Down the hall. Up the hall. Down the hall. Back to his room. His closet door opened. His closet door slammed shut. More frantic feet down the hall.

No one was crying, so that was good. But something was definitely up. Crystal tiptoed up the basement stairs hoping she could see what Paxton was doing without startling or embarrassing him.

From the top of the stairs she hears—

"OH NO! Nooo. Son of a bitch. It was supposed to be a fart. No. Ahhhh, my skateboard. MY SKATEBOARD! NO!"

Crystal turned the corner to enter the living room and was greeted by poop. Lots and lots of poop.

Poop on the hardwood. Poop on the area rug. Poop on Paxton's pants, which were not on him, but flung on the floor. Poop on the walls. Poop on the baseboards. Poop on Paxton. Poop all over his skateboard. And, maybe the only adorable part of this picture, poop all jammed up in his toy vacuum cleaner.

Crystal, somehow, managed to take a picture of the mess. She captioned the pic, "How's your day going?" and sent it to me. She returned her attention to a poopy pantless Paxton.

CRYSTAL: What happened, buddy?

PAXTON: Please don't take my skateboard away. I had an accident.

CRYSTAL: It's ok. I won't. Can you tell me what happened?

PAXTON: Well...I was skateboarding...

CRYSTAL: Ok.

PAXTON: ...and I farted...

CRYSTAL: Ok.

PAXTON: ...and I farted but it was poop and I was skateboarding and the poop musta fell out of my pants and landed on the floor and then I turned my skateboard and popped a wheelie and hit it with the wheels and then my skateboard slipped and I fell and saw the poop and wanted to clean it up so you didn't see it. I took my pants off and tried to pick up my poop but it was all soft and got smashed and then I picked up my skateboard but it had poop on it and then I got poop on me so I got my vacuum cleaner because your vacuum is downstairs and tried to suck it all up but that didn't work and now there's poop in my vacuum and it won't turn on. And my skateboard has poop all over it. And the rug has poop. The floor poop. Just poop. The fart was poop. Sorry.

CRYSTAL: It's ok Paxton. It was an accident. Daddy has them too. Thank you for trying to help but you can stop trying to clean it up now. I'll start you a bath and then come back to *this*.

PAXTON: But my skateboard. Don't throw it away!

CRYSTAL: I won't. I'm going to clean it for you.

PAXTON: Thanks Mom! I love you.

CRYSTAL: And I love you.

The poopy skateboard incident hit Paxton's confidence hard. It was like diarrhea season all over again but worse. He couldn't get back into pooping on the potty. His toddler logic had his subconscious convinced more than ever—If I'm going to poop my pants then I might as well do it in a diaper.

A week of all-poop accidents followed. It was rough. Paxton's confidence was toast.

It was hard to see him that way, so he and I had a Father-Son chat one night as I was changing what I hoped to be his last diaper.

ME: Hey Paxton.

PAXTON: Hey Dad.

ME: You're almost three. And I know you can do this. You were doing so good for so long.

PAXTON: Then I got sick.

ME: Yeah, but now you're not sick.

PAXTON: But what if I get sick again?

ME: You can't live your life worrying about what ifs, but if you get sick, again, then Mommy and me will take care of you and make sure you feel better.

PAXTON: I don't want to use the potty ever again. I want to wear diapers for the rest of my life.

ME: Well, you can't do that.

PAXTON: Why?

ME: Diapers are for babies and you're a big boy with a skateboard, dude.

PAXTON: Why?

ME: You don't need them anymore.

PAXTON: Why?

ME: Uh, well you're at that age where you stop wearing diapers.

PAXTON: Why?

ME: Because I don't want to wipe poop off your butt anymore.

Joke's on me, kids don't master butt-wiping for a while!

PAXTON: Why?

ME: If you wear diapers all the time and constantly crap your pants then you won't ever be able to grow up and get a girlfriend. At least not the type of girlfriend that you'd want to bring home and introduce to your mother and me.

PAXTON: ...

ME: ...

PAXTON: Ok. I'll use the potty.

And he did. No more accidents after that conversation.

I look forward to sharing this story with his first girlfriend. I'll introduce myself and thank her for the potty training motivation. At first she'll be confused. Then she'll laugh and Paxton will say, "Oh my God. Daaaaaad! Stop!"

Take PICS first.

When your child is in a pickle always take photos before helping.
Unless it's life threatening.

Dan's DADVICE

"Whatcha doin' boys?"
We're building a jump! they said.
"You call that a jump?!"

♡ A HAIKU FROM HUSBAND TO WIFE ♡

"MOM! MOM! MOM! COME QUICK!"
"Why is your father crying?"
"HE WENT OFF OUR JUMP!"

♡ A HAIKU FROM HUSBAND TO WIFE ♡

2016

chapter

7

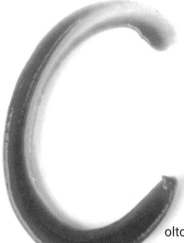olton is pretty much a Sour Patch Kid—first he's sour, then he's sweet.

His little body is jam-packed with emotion. His mind operates on another level. I'm fairly certain he's a savant in the making. He's walking proof of reincarnation. One conversation with Colton and you'll realize he's lived a previous life. Or several of them.

There are a few things you should know about Colton.

First, He's twenty months younger than Paxton. He walked before he crawled. And, the dude skipped baby food. Colton went straight from the boob to hot dogs.

Colton is convinced he's a ninja or a superhero vigilante hell-bent on destroying the most evil manifestation on the planet—bow ties. We once asked him to wear a bow tie for pictures with Santa. At first he didn't say anything, he just looked at it. Then he gently took it from my hand and shouted, "I HATE BOW TIES THEY'RE UGLY, NOT VERY COOL AND FOR BABIES! GET THAT BOW TIE OUTTA MY FACE! PUNCH IT! PUNCH THE BOW TIE IN THE FACE! STOMP ON THE BOW TIE! GO TO SLEEP, BOW TIE!"

He then wrestled the bow tie to the ground and put it in a sleeper hold. He did wear the bow tie for the pictures but not by choice. He was not happy.

Colton also hates angels because quote, "they're big dumb babies," though he has yet to fight one for being in his presence.

His distaste for angels can be traced back to a Christmas ornament he had to make in preschool. His class took pictures and cut their heads out to make an angel ornament. Colton hates things that mess with his face. This is why he avoids Snapchat filters like the plague while his brothers love to send silly Snaps to Grammy.

Colton hates being called cute. I will elaborate on this later.

Colton does what he wants and won't be told otherwise. That's why he leaves the house dressed as Wolverine a lot.

Colton loves his family and everything about being in his family. He constantly tells us so. He is actually a sweetheart but don't EVER let him hear you call him that.

Paxton and Colton are incredibly close, both in relationship and age. Brotherly love is very, very real in our home. So, when Colton and Paxton learned that they were both going to be big brothers they exploded with excitement.

Colton bear-hugged Paxton and shouted, "I'M GOING TO BE A BIG BROTHER JUST LIKE YOU AND YOU'RE GOING TO BE A BIG BROTHER AGAIN!"

The two of them then immediately devised a plan to make room for the new addition.

PAXTON: We need bunk beds!

COLTON: Yeah bunk beds!

PAXTON: You need to move into my room so the baby can have

PAXTON (cont.): the nursery after Mom poops it out. My room will be our room now!

COLTON: Ok! Let's go move my toys into our new room!

THE BOYS IN UNISON: CAN YOU GUYS GET US BUNK BEDS?!

At this time, Colton was two and in a crib while three-year-old Paxton just finished potty training.

CRYSTAL: Absolutely! Bunk beds would be perfect. But Colton, that means no more crib for you.

COLTON: Yeah, yeah. I'm a big brother. Cribs are for babies. I'm not a baby anymore, remember?

That weekend the boys agreed on a paint color and went to Grammy and Pap-Pap's while Crystal and I built bunk beds, painted their room and artfully decorated the space with new toy storage, books and robots.

They were so pumped. Their genuine reactions to the idea of another sibling brought a tear to my eye. Not only were they eager to welcome a new baby into our home but they provided rave reviews on their new shared space.

"THE BEST AND HAPPIEST ROOM EVER!" - Paxton

"THIS ACTUALLY MAKES ME WANT TO GO TO SLEEP!" - Colton

Moments before their first night in their new Big Bro Bunk Suite.

COLTON: Mom, now that I'm going to be a big brother and I have

COLTON (cont.): my own big boy bed I need to tell you something.

CRYSTAL: What's that, buddy?

COLTON: Diapers are for babies.

CRYSTAL: Ok.

COLTON: I'm not a baby anymore. I don't want to wear them. I want to use the potty like my big brother, Paxton, you know since I'm a big brother with a big boy bed.

Crystal looks at me.

CRYSTAL: What do you think, Dad?

ME: Uhhhhh sure. Why not? Let's ditch that diaper in the morning, after one more night.

COLTON: Nope. I want it off now.

And in that moment I witness Colton put diapers in the number three slot on his shitlist, behind bow ties and angels.

CRYSTAL: Ok. No more diapers.

COLTON: No more diapers.

And that was the last diaper Colton ever wore. He woke up dry the next morning, made it through the entire day accident-free and woke up the following morning dry, again.

I've had more accidents than him since then.

Sweet baby Jesus,
fucked up my back on that jump.
IBUPROFEN NOW!

♡ A HAIKU FROM HUSBAND TO WIFE ♡

2017

chapter

8

commitment

utterflies.

Yeah, butterflies. They're to blame for this one. Stupid butterflies.

Paxton was starting kindergarten. He absolutely loved preschool and completed two strenuous years of finger painting and snack time, plus learned valuable early life skills like introducing himself to new friends. The kid oozed (and is still oozing) confidence.

It's pretty remarkable how he can just chat anyone up. I've seen him get shy kids out of their shells and sad kids to laugh. He dressed as a slice of pizza for Halloween two years in a row because "everyone loves pizza."

In fact, the second Halloween I watched him very quickly charm a group of middle school girls. One saw his costume and exclaimed, "OMG! Pizza! I love pizza!"

Pax looked at me knowingly. "See, Dad? I told you everyone *loves* pizza."

He walked up to them and in no time had the girls laughing. He then escorted the entire group down the sidewalk to the next house to collect candy.

Meanwhile, he left his little brother Colton behind.

"Paxton!" I called out. "You forgot about Colton."

Before Paxton could respond (I doubt he even heard me) Colton stormed toward the house.

"DAD! I keep telling you! I'm not Colton. When the mask is on I am Wolverine. When the mask is off, I am Logan. Does it look like I have the mask on? No! I am Logan!"

I stood there in disbelief until a sudden realization hit me—Paxton was ready to board the school bus and rule the elementary school, while Wolverine Colton (sorry Logan Colton) was still focused on trick-or-treating on Graymalkin Lane.

They grow up so fast. This whole school thing is going to be a cakewalk, right?

Not so fast there, lover boy.

'Twas the night before the first day of kindergarten annnnnnd the butterflies set in. Big time. Paxton was quiet. Timid. Avoiding eye contact. Looking down at his plate. I could see the jitters setting in. It was an important reminder that he was still a child, despite his outward display of confidence.

But Paxton wouldn't admit that he was feeling nervous or anxious. Those words are not in his vocabulary. So that night at dinner when he began retreating into his shell, I knew he wasn't going to admit how he was feeling. I needed to carefully pry information out of him.

All three boys were sitting at the table eating corn dogs and ketchup—two of the five basic food groups in our home. The others are ranch dressing, chicken nuggets and mac and cheese.

Actually, Greyson was standing because he refuses to sit and eat. That kid never sits. He was double fisting corn dogs that night and got really into it, so we just let him do his thing.

I noticed Paxton wasn't really eating his corn dog but more so just mashing pieces of it into the mound of ketchup on his plate. Red flag. He was nervous about his big day tomorrow. Totally understandable. It was time to share another Father-Son chat.

ME: Hey dude, what's up?

PAXTON: Goooooood.

That's his typical answer to this question even though it doesn't really answer the question.

ME: Is something on your mind?

PAXTON: I dunno.

ME: Well, what are you thinking about?

PAXTON: School.

ME: What about it?

PAXTON: I dunno.

ME: Are you excited?

PAXTON: Oh yeah! I can't wait to ride the bus!

ME: Anything else?

PAXTON: Yeah...

I nod and gesture in an effort get him to elaborate.

PAXTON: Do I know anyone in my class?

ME: You know a couple of kids. Remember orientation? Luke up the street is in your class. And you went to school last year with Nora, and Trey who you met at orientation.

COLTON: Dad, a couple is two and you named three kids.

I peer into the soul of my smartass son. He is confidently amused with himself.

ME: That's correct, Colton. Great job focusing on the details.

PAXTON: Oh yeah! But what if I don't meet anyone else? What if no one wants to talk to me?

ME: Dude. You're pizza. Everyone loves pizza, right?

PAXTON: I'm pizza? Oh yeah. That's right!

ME: Plus, you never know who you will meet on your first day of kindergarten. Did you know that Mommy and I met on the first day of kindergarten?

PAXTON AND COLTON: What?!?!

GREYSON: (screams in solidarity with his brothers)

PAXTON: You and Mommy met in kindergarten?!

ME: Yup.

PAXTON: Woooooooow.

The conversation stopped there. I could tell Paxton felt better about his upcoming first day. He smiled at Crystal and I, then jammed five fingers into his ketchup pile and finished eating his corn dog.

Fast forward to 3:20 the next afternoon. Crystal, Colton, Greyson and I were at Paxton's bus stop. He got off the bus wearing a massive shit-eating grin. He had a great day.

Paxton shared every exciting detail over the next couple of hours. The majority of the conversation went as expected. His teacher was awesome! His lunch was great! He met all these new friends and played outside for recess! He has gym tomorrow and has to wear gym clothes!

The conversation slowed down and Paxton sat down on the couch to watch Netflix.

Forty-five minutes later

"OH. I FORGOT TO TELL YOU. I HAVE A GIRLFRIEND."

ME: Really?

PAXTON: Yup!

ME: Tell us about her! What's her name?

PAXTON: Ummmmm. I don't know her name. But she is a super sweet girl and is in my class. Today, when I got to class I put my backpack in my cubby and saw Trey and Luke so I said, "Hey guys! What's up? Good to see you." And we were just talking and hanging out as I put my backpack in my backpack cubby and I look over my right shoulder and then I saw her. Just standing there. She was wearing...like jeans...like the pants, but they weren't pants and it was a jacket.

CRYSTAL: You mean a jean jacket?

PAXTON: Yeah, yeah, yeah. That's it, a jean jacket! She was wearing a jean jacket. So I looked over my shoulder, like I said, and there she is. Just standing there. And I said to myself, "Oh my God. She is stunning." So I talked to her and told her, "Hi I'm Paxton. What's your name?" But I don't remember her name. And we just played, like all day. She sits next to me and I just really liked her right away. We ate lunch together. We played outside at recess together. I told her I liked her. She said she liked me. Ahhh, it was great. Then we get back to class, I looked at her and say, "Hey. I like you and you like me. Would you like to marry me? Like when we are grown-ups of course?"

CRYSTAL: Ooook. And what did she say?

PAXTON: She looked at me like this...

Paxton stares straight ahead with blank expression on his face.

PAXTON: ...and she said, "Uh, I don't think I'm ready for that so can we just be friends?" And I told her, "Ok. That's cool. Can you pass me the red crayon?" Then we laughed and colored.

ME: Maybe tomorrow you start with remembering her name and just navigate the friendzone for like the next twelve to eighteen years before getting *too* serious.

PAXTON: But you met Mom when you were five.

ME: Yes! You are correct, but I didn't tell Mom I liked her until I was like fifteen. You got time to figure that stuff out.

PAXTON: FIFTEEN?! That's like so far away. I'll just tell her now so she knows and can think about it for a while.

ME: I guess you can do that but please remember your future wife's name.

PAXTON: I got time to figure that stuff out.

Like father, like son. But the biggest difference between the two of us—Paxton can talk to girls already. At that age I would've just run away or avoided them all together.

So, thank you Jean Jacket Girl for the potty training motivation. I wasn't expecting to hear about you so soon.

HEY GOOGLE, HOW DO YOU SPELL PENIS PENIS PENIS PENIS PENIS PENIS PENIS PENIS PENIS?
PENIS PENIS PEN
PENIS PENIS IS SP
E-N-I-S-P-E-N-I-S-
N-I-S-P-E-N-I-S

2017

chapter

9

O ut of the mouth of babes" is the biblical version of "kids say the darndest things." I honestly didn't know what that meant until I wrote this chapter. I had to Google it a few times before it hit me—*that* saying is *this* story in a nutshell.

Kids absorb everything around them. They're like cultural sponges, observing and dissecting the world through a lens of innocence. They connect dots that adults often overlook and they'll tell you exactly what they think in any given circumstance. Their unapologetic opinions and points of view are remarkable, alarming and fucking hilarious.

Explaining what an opinion even is to a child is difficult for two reasons. First, by the time you realize an opinion conversation is necessary he or she has formed their own opinion about opinions. Second, kids know everything about everything. Silly Dad, you'll have better luck turning peanut butter into a diamond than convincing them otherwise.

The opinion paradox occurs between birth and age five. And thanks to the wonders of modern technology and social retargeting, subliminally absorbing information is happening more rapidly.

You can't filter everything. Some questionable content will trickle through and their little minds will absorb and dissect it to the best of their ability. Sometimes that questionable content is a parent's own behavior.

Keep that in mind the next time someone cuts you off in traffic, or you'll be explaining what the traffic finger is, and why preschool is not the appropriate place to show it off. My bad.

So, I've learned that when you mess up, admit fault. It's an opportunity to teach them right from wrong and help mold them into the type of person you want to see in the world.

Remarkably, the older boys (Paxton and Colton) do pay attention to current events, like who is president, what they said in a news clip or what they saw/heard on a retargeted ad on YouTube.

Paxton asks me a lot why our President is so mean-sounding. He sees how Donald Trump presents himself and represents our country on TV and he can see that he isn't following the same rules that he's taught at home and in school—Treat others the way you want to be treated. Use your manners. Be respectful. Never make fun of someone who is different than you.

This is a hard one to answer, not because he is five but because he is five and sees something wrong. But, not all of his political questions are as tough.

"WHY DOES THAT LADY LOOK LIKE A CAN OF PEPSI BUT WITHOUT THE LOGO?" he asked once.

I looked up at the TV and saw he was referring to Hillary Clinton and her signature all blue pant suit.

I tell the boys these questions are always welcomed at home, but I advise them to avoid talking politics with friends and family as they grow up. "As they grow up" being the key phrase there. I said it, but Colton interpreted that differently—because he's not grown up, yet.

One summer our family of five joined my parents at their camp for the weekend. Pap-Pap and Grammy took us fishing, we spent some time on Aunt Nickie and Uncle Eric's boat and made s'mores at the fire every night. It was a nice weekend for extended family bonding.

Saturday morning I wake to a conversation between Colton, Crystal and Grammy at the kitchen table in the camper.

COLTON: You know, Grammy. I really miss Sundae.

Sundae was Grammy and Pap-Pap's chocolate lab. She was fourteen and had to be put to sleep because her health was deteriorating. She was a great dog and a close companion to everyone.

GRAMMY: I'm sorry. I know, sweetie. I do too. She loved you very much.

COLTON: Yeah. I know. I love her. I just wish she was here.

GRAMMY: It's ok. She isn't in pain anymore though. And that's good, right?

COLTON: I dunno, it's just not fair. I think she was fine.

GRAMMY: I'm sorry, Colton. She loved playing with you and I know she loved staying at your house a couple of weeks ago.

COLTON: I just wish she was here. I want to play with her.

GRAMMY: I'm sorry.

COLTON: I know. I know. I know. You keep saying I'm sorry. But my opinion is I wish she was here.

Grammy chuckles at how animated he is.

GRAMMY: I know buddy.

COLTON: Don't laugh at me, please. You're starting to act like that guy on TV.

CRYSTAL: The guy on TV?

Crystal and Grammy exchange glances, not sure where this is going.

COLTON: Yeah. You know the guy on TV?

CRYSTAL: Which guy, Colton? There are a lot of guys on TV.

GRAMMY: What does he look like?

COLTON: Ugh. You know, the guy that's always yelling!

GRAMMY: That doesn't really narrow it down. What's he look like?

COLTON: He's the guy who is always yelling and tells everyone, "I'm right! You're wrong!" That's his opinion, he's always saying his opinion is right. He does this with his face.

Colton wrinkles his brow, squints his eyes and puckers his lips into a tight butthole shape. He holds his right hand out and points his index finger before slamming his hand down on the table.

Grammy softly laughs at his animated facial expressions.

COLTON: Stop laughing at me, please.

GRAMMY: Sorry, sweetie. What does this have to do with opinions?

COLTON: Your opinion is SHE WAS OLD AND I'M SORRY. My opinion is I MISS HER.

I get a feeling this is about to get real.

CRYSTAL: Ok. What else do you know about this guy? What does he wear?

COLTON: Mom! You know who this is, he's the guy that's always yelling that he's right!

CRYSTAL: You keep saying that but what does he look like?

COLTON: He wears a red tie!

Shit. I know who he's talking about.

ME: Are you talking about Donald Trump?

COLTON: YEAH! YEAH, THAT'S RIGHT! THE PRESIDENT! He's always saying that he is right. Always yelling about how he is right. Telling everyone else, "WRONG. FAKE. BLAH BLAH BLAH."

GRAMMY: Well, can't we both be right?

COLTON: Yeah...I guess so. But I still miss Sundae.

2017

chapter

10

Kids can't wait to grow up. I always wanted to be big, then reality hit sometime in my late twenties. I realized mortgages suck and summer vacations were no longer a thing. But hey, now I'm a parent and stay vicariously young through Greyson, Colton and Paxton.

I do, more than occasionally, like to remind my kids to not rush growing up. There's plenty of time to be a grown-up when you actually grow up. Slow down and enjoy this time in your life when it's cute and acceptable to pee outside.

But still each boy loves to talk about what their life will be like when they're old, fat and drink beer like Dad. Thanks guys, I love you too.

Paxton typically sticks to common themes—love, marriage and work. He talks about this sweet girl with green eyes and brown hair (who probably wears a jean jacket) that he is going to marry, and how they will raise a family together in a house with a red roof with a nice big yard. He talks in length about his career as a construction worker, the number of jobs he'll work on and the type of machinery he'll run.

He insists he will drive a concrete mixer. Not only as a work truck but for everything. Commuting, grocery shopping, cruising around, visiting Mom and Dad since we'll be "old, lonely and bored in a quiet and empty house."

That's a pretty unrealistic goal I think. A concrete mixer for your daily driver? What about parking and gas? But of course he has an answer for that.

"I'll park it wherever I want because it's so huge no one can move it," he'll say. And "I'll have a job so I can buy gas, duh." Touché, Pac Man, touché.

Greyson, AKA Danger Baby, is a friggin' lunatic. I swear 90% of the time Crystal, Paxton, Colton and I are trying to prevent him from killing himself and/or tearing the house down. The other 10% of the time is split between YouTube Kids, superhero movies and pointing at our Google Home. That means he wants to dance to music.

Danger Baby's taste in music includes The Ramones, Rage Against the Machine, Elvis Costello, The Aquabats, System of a Down and Baby Shark doo doo doo doo doo doo.

Like most babies he's fascinated with the toilet. When Danger Baby runs down the hall empty-handed you know what he's up to. The moment he rounds the living room corner to the hall you have four seconds to stop him. FOUR. SECONDS. At five his arms are filled with toys, clothes, bottles, the part of the remote that *was* missing for three days, miscellaneous valuables annnnnd into the shitter they go.

I know. I know. They make locks for toilets but he just rips them off and chucks those in the can, too. Plus potty locks with a three and five-year-old can be disastrous. I'll take fishing for things over mopping up pee any day.

Danger Baby also eats toilet paper and headbutts walls if you tell him, "'NO! DON'T EAT DOO DOO PAPER, DANGER BABY!" Danger Baby is punk rock and doesn't give a shit so he'll eat the doo doo paper and laugh at you for trying to stop him.

Go ahead and try to clean up the mess in the bathroom. He'll run to the kitchen, open the oven door and jump on it like a trampoline. He also tries to climb into the oven when he's bored.

It's never on when he does that. Just thought I'd clarify so no one calls CPS on me.

Honestly, Crystal and I should have purchased stock in baby gates. Baby gates go up in our home at an alarming rate. Gate in the hallway. Gate in the kitchen. Gate in the living room. Our home at one point looked like a maximum security prison.

But The Barriers of Prevention only do so much. Greyson still finds ways to wreak havoc. Scaling the (electric) fireplace, dancing on the dining room table, jumping off anything and everything in sight, yelling. Loud, sustained, powerful yelling for hours on end.

If I had to put money on Greyson's future profession then it'd be a toss up between the reigning champion on Supermarket Sweep or America Ninja Warrior. If that falls through then he has a future as the crazy guy downtown who yells at buildings. Right now, it's unfortunately just too soon to tell.

Then there's Colton. Colton has a lot of ideas about what Grown Up Colton's life will consist of. His imagination runs the gamut when asked what he wants to be. Anything from Just Myself to Wolverine to "Stop asking me that question, Dad. Can't you see I'm a teenager?"

Colton never gives the same two answers but his answers are always either profound or completely batshit crazy. Every parent says stuff like my kid is so smart because of this or that relatively mundane thing they said or did. Colton, however, is the kid that makes me stop and wonder if he hasn't already figured out this whole life thing at the tender age of three.

GROWNUP COLTON no.1

COLTON: Mom, when I grow up I don't want to get married.

CRYSTAL: That's totally fine. You don't have to get married.

COLTON: I just don't want that.

CRYSTAL: Ok. What do you want?

COLTON: I want to ride a green motorcycle with my cat, Kitty Kat Kitty Kat, and just live free. No responsibilities. No worries. Just me, Kitty Kat Kitty Kat and the open road. Yeah. That's the life.

GROWNUP COLTON no.2

COLTON: Hey Dad, when I grow up I want to be a rhino.

ME: Dude! When I grow up I want to be a rhino too!

COLTON: Well, you can't be a rhino. You're already grown up. You're just a normal dad.

ME: Uhhhh, in that case you can't be a rhino either. It's impossible. Rhinos are an entirely different species than humans. How are you going to become a rhino?

Without missing a beat Colton stand up, throws his head back and raises his hands as if he is harnessing the power of a hundred suns. He charges at me and shouts.

COLTON: RHINOOOOOOO POWWWWW-ERRRRRRR ACTI-VAAAAAAAAAAATE!!!!!!!

ME: HOLY CRAP YOU'RE A RHINO!

COLTON: See? I told you I could be a rhino when I grow up. I'm just getting started.

GROWNUP COLTON no.3

COLTON: When I grow up, I'll come back to visit you two when you're old and smelly, but I'll make my girlfriend stay in the car.

CRYSTAL: She doesn't have to stay in the car.

COLTON: Yes she does! And if she doesn't listen then I'm going to hit her in the head with a hammer.

ME: COLTON! NO! Never hit your girlfriend. NEVER HIT A GIRL. Especially with a hammer. I don't want to hear you say something that terrible again.

COLTON: Ok.

ME: Do I hit Mommy?

COLTON: No.

ME: You understand how bad what you just said was, right?

COLTON: Yeah. Sorry. I won't hit my girlfriend. In the head. With a hammer.

ME: Thank you.

COLTON: Can I finish my story now?

ME: Yes, absolutely.

COLTON: So as I was saying, when I grow up, I'll come back to visit you two when you're old and smelly, but I'll make my girl...

He stops and looks me dead in the eyes.

COLTON: ...boyfriend stay in the car and if he doesn't listen then I'm going to hit him in the head with a hammer.

ME: COLTON BROOX!

COLTON: What?!

── {̊ *huh* }̊ ──

Sorry, what was that?
I swear. I was listening.
Okay. I wasn't.

♡ A HAIKU FROM HUSBAND TO WIFE ♡

HELL
is
Parenting
with a
hangover.

Dan's
Dadvice

2016

chapter

11

EXOTIC Palettes

etting kids to eat new things is almost impossible. I'm not joking when I say the five basic food groups in our home are corn dogs, ketchup, ranch dressing, chicken nuggets, and mac and cheese.

There's also the Snack Box. I forgot to mention that earlier. That's like our sixth food group, the junk food portion of our pyramid. Yes, it's exactly what it sounds like—a big box filled with assorted snacks. WE LOVE THE SNACK BOX!

I know some of you more pretentious parents are judging me right now. Re-fucking-lax. There's one thing these boys love more than the Snack Box and that's brushing their teeth. And that passion started with the first tooth. I don't know why but they looooooove brushing their teeth. So there. Dental hygiene for the win.

Oh, and pizza. The boys love pizza, too. Pizza is an easy win for dinner.

So, we have five (or six) food groups and three strict food rules in our home.

1. Try it. More times than not, a new food is well-received. That's how Greyson discovered brisket and tri-tip. Honestly, he's not a picky eater. He's a garbage disposal. So this chapter doesn't pertain to him. Yet.

2. No one goes to bed hungry. Doesn't matter how late it is, there's always time for cereal.

3. Ask to be excused from the table, and stay at the table when eating. Nothing sucks more than watching kids run around at a restaurant. Manners start at home.

Still, getting them (Paxton and Colton) to eat new things is difficult. We often rely on the five basic food groups with a glass of milk or one of Mom's fresh fruit smoothies.

So it was really unexpected when Colton came out of left field with a specific dinner request—Dolphin. But not just any dolphin, fresh-caught and butchered dolphin. Both of which he swore he could do himself.

I didn't think he even knew what a dolphin was or what they looked like. They're not exactly animals we talk a lot about, and he's never watched *Flipper* or *The Cove*. The request for this exotic meat was, and still is, one of Colton's stranger moments.

COLTON: Hey guys!?

PARENTS IN UNISON: Yeeeees?

COLTON: I'm hungry. When can we go to the beach?

ME: Would you like me to make you something or do you want something from the Snack Box?

COLTON: Ummm, when can we go to the beach?

CRYSTAL: We will have to plan a family vacation to the beach. The beach is a pretty long car ride so we will take a few trips before that to see how you guys do in the car.

COLTON: But I'm hungry.

ME: Ok, if you're hungry then would you like me to make you something or do you want something from the Snack Box?

COLTON: No, thank you.

ME: Ok. Are you hungry for something in particular? Waffles, pizza, mac and—

COLTON: Yes.

ME: Ok. Which one?

COLTON: No.

ME: What?

COLTON: Dolphin.

ME: What?

COLTON: I'm hungry for dolphin.

PARENTS IN UNISON: What?

"I. WANT. TO. EAT. A. DOL. PHIN." He said slowly, syllable by syllable.

ME: What?

COLTON: I said I WANT TO EAT A DOLPHIN, DAD! Come on, can you hear me?

ME: Oh I can hear you, Colton. I'm just confused. You want to eat a dolphin?

COLTON: YES!

ME: You can't eat a dolphin.

COLTON: And why not?

ME: Well for one, I'm pretty sure dolphin meat is illegal in the United States or at the very least extremely frowned upon.

COLTON: HEY GOOGLE, IS DOLPHIN MEAT ILLEGAL?

GOOGLE HOME: I don't know that yet but I'm always learning.

Thanks for the backup, Google.

ME: And two, dolphin meat is not good for you. It's very high in mercury.

COLTON: Mercury? Like the planet? Dad, how the heck does an entire planet get into a dolphin?

ME: No, not the planet. Mercury is a chemical.

COLTON: A chemical?

ME: Yes, a chemical. It's a pollutant that runs off into the ocean and makes the water dirty. Fish and other creatures absorb the chemicals, then dolphins eat those fish and it makes them not safe to eat.

COLTON: I still want to try dolphin. You always say TRY IT and see if you like it.

ME: You're right but this is different. We can't just go to the grocery store and pick up a chunk of dolphin meat.

COLTON: Duh. That's why I want to go to the beach.

ME: Elaborate, please.

COLTON: I want to go to the beach so I can jump in the water and swim out really far in the ocean until I find a dolphin then when I find a dolphin I'll jump on it and fight it and it will fight back. And we will fight each other. Then I'll punch it. BAM! Sleeper hold! So now I got it in a sleeper hold and I'm gonna punch it in the blowhole again and again like this.

He puts an imaginary dolphin in a sleeper hold and leg locks its body. Then he proceeds to punch it in the blowhole.

COLTON: Then the dolphin will be dead or like too tired to fight and I'll swim back to the beach with the tail in my mouth. I'll drag it out of the water and eat it right there on the beach with a side of ranch dressing, you know for dipping.

ME: But you can't swim.

COLTON: I'll learn.

ME: And how are you going to cook it?

COLTON: I'll cook it right there on the beach with my microwave. I'll have a big bottle of ranch dressing with me, you know for dipping.

CRYSTAL: Yeah, you can't just hook a microwave up on the beach. And you can't kill a dolphin. That's just not a nice thing to do. Plus that's definitely illegal and your actions will have consequences.

ME: (whispering to her) Well, dolphins are sorta huge assholes. I've seen videos of them doing terrible things.

She shoots me a death stare.

CRYSTAL: No.

COLTON: Fine. Fine. Fine. I'll just starve.

Colton's appetite for dolphin did not end there. For weeks he would subtly suggest that maybe we try something new for dinner. Like a new kind of mac and cheese or something else like, "Oh, I don't know. Dolphin?"

Every time Colton brought dolphin up he would plead, "Please, let's just go to the beach so I can catch one. You'll see how good it is. Trust me."

We weren't going to the beach anytime soon. The last thing I wanted was for my three-year-old to drown or catch a felony charge trying to murder a dolphin with his bare hands.

But still, he would request dolphin. Dolphin steak. Dolphin nuggets. Dolphin tail. Dolphin fries. Any kind of dolphin meal imaginable. After a few months of dolphin talk I decided to give the kid what he was asking for—a super exclusive †Dolphin Sandwich®.

It was around noon on a Saturday in November. The air was crisp and chilly, just like I imagine a dolphin fillet would be. All three boys were in the back seat of the car. Crystal was driving and I rode shotgun. We were hungry and needed something fast.

Over an hour had passed since the last time the kids ate something. A weird look began to consume their eyes. They started gnawing on one another. Images of the Donner Party danced in my head. Eating your brother is a bad thing. Typically.

Paxton wanted McDonald's. Greyson wanted anything he could reach, hence the chewing on his brothers. Colton wanted dolphin. We are wonderful parents, so naturally we ignored their requests and pulled into Chick-fil-A since that's what we wanted. And it was the closest drive-thru.

"BUT WE DON'T LIKE CHICK-FIL-A!" the boys protested.

"Bullshit. You fucking like it," I said to myself. In my head. They must have forgotten this place has waffle fries.

We ordered an abundance of chicken sandwiches, nuggets, waffle fries and †*one super exclusive Dolphin Sandwich®* with a side of ranch dressing.

When Colton heard me order one super exclusive Dolphin Sandwich® his eyes widened.

"NO. EFFING. WAY," he said. "They have that here?"

"Yup. They sure do, buddy. For a limited time only. Don't tell the government, ok?"

"Ok. I won't tell the government."

We got home, sat down at the table as a family and ate. For the first time Colton tried "dolphin" and more importantly, finished his entire sandwich.

Seriously, he never eats anything (besides waffle fries) from Chick-fil-A. It was a pre-Christmas miracle. And just like that, his insatiable hunger for dolphin was fulfilled.

For now.

" THIS IS THE BEST DAY OF MY LIFE. " - Colton, after finally eating dolphin

†Chick-fil-A does not and never will serve a super exclusive Dolphin Sandwich® with or without a side of ranch. It was a normal chicken sandwich. I lied to my child and he believed it. What a sucker!

Just ONCE make good on a threat

Shop Vac up the Legos, turn the car around, "leave" the house without them and watch the panic set in as they realize your words actually mean something.

Dan's DADVICE

I'm on my way home.
"That's great. Can you pick up milk?"
I'm home. "Where's the milk?"

♡ A HAIKU FROM HUSBAND TO WIFE ♡

Walk in the front door.
"You forgot the milk, again."
Walk back out the door.

♡ A HAIKU FROM HUSBAND TO WIFE ♡

2017

chapter

12

Lying to your kids to trick them into eating doesn't always work. Eventually they catch on and realize the dolphin in their super exclusive Dolphin Sandwich® was actually chicken and they stop speaking to you for day or so because you "broke their heart" or some mumbo jumbo like that.

The silent treatment isn't a punishment for a parent. It's a reward. A very, very short-lived reward. If you want your kid(s) to start talking to you again then just sit down and put your feet up. They will not sit by as you relax. Before you know it you'll hear stuff like—

PAXTON: I gotta poop.

COLTON: What's your favorite color?

PAXTON: Where's Mom?

COLTON: Have you seen my mask?

PAXTON: Where's Mom?

ME: She's literally sitting right next to me.

COLTON: I'm hot.

PAXTON: I'm cold.

COLTON: Can I wear shorts?

PAXTON: If he's wearing shorts then I want shorts too.

COLTON: Why do you fart so much?

PAXTON: Mom doesn't fart.

COLTON: When's Mom going to be home?

ME: She's home. Again, she's literally sitting right next to me. You can see her.

PAXTON: Are you sleeping?

COLTON: Are you dead?

Paxton pokes me in the eye.

PAXTON: Can I have a snack?

COLTON: Do we have any corn dogs?

PAXTON: Can I have a corn dog?

COLTON: I'm hungry.

PAXTON: I'm hungry, too.

COLTON: I'm like really really hungry.

PAXTON: Did you hear me?

COLTON: Food!? Yeah! Hello?

PAXTON: Does my finger smell funny?

CRYSTAL: *(sniffs finger)* OH MY GOD! What did you do?

PAXTON: Well, you see, my butt was itchy...

CRYSTAL: Ok. I'm up. Bathroom now. Your hands need washed and your butt needs re-wiped.

COLTON: But I'm hungry.

CRYSTAL: Yeah and your brother's hands smell like death. We're all washing our hands while Dad makes corn dogs for lunch.

COLTON: But I don't want the corn part.

ME: So, a hot dog?

COLTON: Yeah. With ranch, you know for dipping.

PAXTON: Yeah, no corn on my corn dog. With lots of ketchup, not ranch, for dipping.

ME: So, a hot dog?

PAXTON: Yeah.

ME: G. Anything you want to add?

GREYSON: Hi Dada!

ME: Hi Greyson.

Fast forward two minutes and thirty seconds. Two cornless corn dogs have been served, with various sauces for dipping.

ME: Why are you two not eating?

PAXTON: I'm not hungry.

COLTON: I'm not hungry, either.

ME: This is why hamsters eat their young. Look at your little brother! He is housing his food.

GREYSON: More please, Dada.

ME: Oh man! G! You ate everything and you want more. Awesome job dude! Best kid of the day!

PAXTON: He can eat mine.

ME: Nope. You can eat yours.

COLTON: Can I be excused?

ME: Nope. You both are going to sit there and eat these cornless corn dogs with ketchup and ranch.

COLTON: But we're not hungry.

ME: Gimme your plates, please. Stay at the table. I'll be right back. I'm going to make G another hot dog.

PAXTON AND COLTON: (panic stricken) What are you doing with our food?!

ME: Shhhh. I'll be right back with your food. Don't leave the table.

As I made my way to the kitchen, my brain rattled off a bunch of argument-winning comebacks to throw at my suddenly not hungry kids. I picture them being immediately shut down by my brilliance, and they begin to eat. Heavenly rays of sunlight illuminate the dining room. Birds chirp outside. We all laugh joyfully. Everything is suddenly in slow motion. My daydream continues to play out in my mind as I ask myself, why do they do this stuff?

Answer—they're kids.

And kids are annoying. They change their minds. Sometimes they legitimately change their minds. Sometimes they change their minds intentionally to get a reaction out of you. They can be diabolical sons of bitches, no offense to my amazingly beautiful and tolerant wife (Love ya babe). Other times they don't know what they want and the only way for them to figure it out is by sputtering out an infinite string of disjointed thoughts until you feel a vein pop in the back of your head.

It makes me wonder how the hell, we as a species, evolved to this point. Do bear cubs refuse to eat? What about baby tigers or alligator kids? I doubt it. We know hamsters eat their young. If I had to guess why then I'd venture to say those little furballs refused to eat the pellets or mealworms they literally just asked Momma Hamster for and then *POP* goes the vein in the back of Momma Hamster's head. She snaps and chows down on her own flesh and blood.

I'm not a goddamn child-eating hamster, but Colton and Paxton were eating those freaking cornless corn dog with ketchup and ranch for dipping whether they wanted to or not. I devised a plan. A game of sorts. Something that encouraged them to eat through imaginative play. Don't play with your food? Poppycock! This is gonna be fun!

I returned to the dining room table with a second helping for Greyson and some modified cornless corn dogs, with fresh ketchup and ranch. G dug in again, without hesitation. Paxton and Colton looked amused and perplexed.

PAXTON: Uhhh, Dad? Why does my hot dog have a face?

COLTON: A face?! Ha! Look at this guy! He looks so happy!

ME: He is happy! And do you know why he's so happy?

PAXTON AND COLTON: No.

ME: He's happy because he's alive!

The boys look down at the hot dogs I've carved innocent smiling faces into.

PAXTON AND COLTON: He's alive!?

ME: Yup. And now we're gonna play a game with him.

PAXTON: A game?

COLTON: OH MAN GAMES ARE AWESOME!

ME: So here's the deal, that isn't a hot dog. It's a person. A really small person who needs a home. Do you think you guys can find him a home?

COLTON: No way! I'm just going to bite his head off!

ME: SHHHH. Don't let him hear you say that. He'll run away. You need to gain his trust before you bite his head off.

PAXTON: But that sounds like a lie. And you always say lying is wrong. I'll just tell him the truth.

Golly gee willikers would ya look at Mr. Literal over here. He does listen!

COLTON: Can't I just tell him that I'm going to bite his head off?

ME: Yeah, go with that. Just tell him you're going to bite his head off and then bite his head off.

The boys shake their heads in agreement and turn their focus to the sacrifice lying in front of them.

PAXTON: Hi, I'm Paxton. I'm going to eat you now. Your new home is in my belly.

COLTON: Nice face, wiener man. Chomp.

Hot damn it actually worked! They ate those godforsaken cornless corn dogs that they were like really, really hungry for. I am the best Dad ever #parentingwin #gome.

Colton and Paxton really enjoyed role-playing with their food and Greyson loved playing alongside his older brothers. It became a regular thing. The dialogue and backstory with every meal and snack became increasingly more complex.

What started with a "Hi, I'm Paxton. I'm going to eat you now," and "Nice face, wiener man," grew into a really weird dining room table stage play. Like *Lord of the Flies* weird. Things got too real too fast and I started to think that encouraging cannibalism was a really bad idea.

DON'T ROLE-PLAY
WITH YOUR FOOD <u>act</u> 1

The laughter of three children echoes throughout our home.
My face drops as I realize it's coming from the bathroom.
I must investigate.

ME: Heeey. Whatcha guys doing in here? It sounds fun.

PAXTON: We're hanging out.

COLTON: And snacking.

Greyson holds a bag of Goldfish, the cracker snack that smiles
back until you bite their heads off.

GREYSON: Boom!

ME: Hanging out and snacking? In the bathroom? That's weird.

COLTON: Not that weird.

ME: Ok. But where are your pants?

PAXTON: Dad, we're hanging out.

ME: Yeah, I see that.

GREYSON: Boom!

The boys burst into laughter.

ME: G. What are you doing?

G turns to me, just realizing I am in the bathroom. G screams and
hides in the bathtub.

GREYSON: OH NO DADA! RUN!

Paxton and Colton are turning red with laughter.

ME: What's so funn—

I piece it all together. Laughter. No pants. Guilty little brother. Goldfish. Bathroom.

ME: Dudes! How many Goldfish did you put in the toilet?

PAXTON AND COLTON: We didn't do it! Greyson did it.

ME: You sold out your own brother?! Greyson, did you do this?

GREYSON: YEAH!

ME: And you two didn't stop him?

COLTON: No. We were making fishy ghosts and eating them.

ME: EATING THEM?! OUT OF THE TOILET?!

COLTON: No! The bag.

ME: I hope these all flush.

They do.

ME: Did you put the entire bag in the toilet?

COLTON: Kinda but we ate some too.

ME: But why don't you have pants on?

PAXTON: We're hanging out.

COLTON: And practicing! Greyson was helping us practice.

ME: Practicing?

PAXTON: Our aim.

COLTON: We were peeing on the fish in the toilet!

ME: Well, you need more practice. You missed. A lot.

DON'T ROLE-PLAY
WITH YOUR FOOD <u>act</u> 2

The sun is masked by a cloudy sky. A young hunter stalks his prey. Life is tough in the Triassic Age. But the harsh conditions only encourage our young hunter. He's hungry and it's lunchtime.

DINO NUGGET: (panicked whispering) Fam-i-ly? Fam-i-ly?

COLTON: What's that, Mr. Dino Nugget?

DINO NUGGET: I can't find my family!

COLTON: You can't find your family? Huh. Weird.

The young hunter pauses to build suspense.

COLTON: Maybe that's because I ate them! (maniacal laughter)

The young hunter shakes the plate startling the lone dino nugget.

COLTON: Just kidding. They're in the cave. Look. Chomp.

He tosses the dino nugget into his mouth.

COLTON: Ha. The cave was my mouth, dummy. Tricked ya! I did eat your family!

DON'T ROLE-PLAY
WITH YOUR FOOD <u>act</u> 3

I've lost track of time. I'm beginning to fear for my life. The natives have proven to be brutal and unrelenting. I fear my days are numbered. Pray for me. Tell my wife I love her.

PAXTON: Colton, gimme the dad one, please.

COLTON: This one?

PAXTON: Yeah. Perfect.

ME: Dudes. They're Oreos. They're all identical.

PAXTON: Nope. This is the dad one. He just got home from work and is sitting in his car. He had a long day and needs a beer and wants to see his family.

Huh, another family. Another fatherly food item.

Pax holds the cookie up for me to inspect.

PAXTON: See how tired he looks?

ME: Thanks, buddy. I love you too.

Oreo Dad begins to make his way from the edge of the table (driveway) to the box of cookies (his home).

PAXTON: Hey you!

OREO DAD (voiced by Paxton): Ah! A GIANT! HELP!

PAXTON: Not so fast.

A cup of milk slides into the scene.

OREO DAD: No!

Dunk.

OREO DAD: I

Dunk.

OREO DAD: Can't

Dunk.

OREO DAD: Swim!

Long dunk.

OREO DAD: I'm dead.

Nom nom nom.

COLTON: Paxton! Look!

OREO MOM (voiced by Colton): Husband? Husband? Are you out here? I thought I heard you?

Oreo Mom looks around.

OREO MOM: Ah! A GIANT! HELP!

Dunk.

OREO MOM: I

Dunk.

OREO MOM: Can't

Dunk.

OREO MOM: Swim!

Long dunk.

OREO MOM: I'm dead too.

Nom nom nom.

OREO KID 1 (voiced by Colton): Mom?

OREO KID 2 (voiced by Paxton): Dad?

OREO KID 1: Mom?

OREO KID 2: Ah! A GIANT! HELP!

Dunk. Dunk. Dunk.

Nom nom nom.

ME: Ok. Slow down before you choke. You have an entire family in your mouth.

They chew slower.

For the first time in my life I felt empathy for food. Those poor helpless hot dogs, dinonuggets, and Oreos. They had families. They just wanted to get home to see them. They didn't deserve this. Did they?

Nah. Effffff that. The kids were eating and having fun doing it. Even if they were making fun of me in the process, it's still a win-win. Plus they were being creative!

I *am* the best Dad ever #parentingwin #gome.

2018

chapter

13

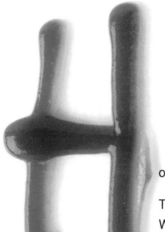

ow does a typical three-year-old act?

That's not a riddle. It's serious question. We've never had one. And judging by Greyson's spitfire personality, we will never have one. Ever. That's just the way our family turned out. But even with all the random and borderline unbelievable stories we have, there are still some moments that surprise us.

Like I mentioned earlier, Colton has a lot of personalities. Any of which can show up without warning, even at school. His teachers not-so-secretly love and embrace this. In fact, they enjoy his stories so much that they often share them with us after class! Oh to be a fly on the wall in his classroom.

Colton begged us to start school when he was one-and-a-half. He saw his older brother, Paxton, experiencing independence for the first time. He wanted that too. He didn't see the anxiety Paxton was having, he just saw an experience that he was missing out on and didn't like being treated different than his brother. Colton cried everyday at drop-off because he wanted to be in class. The preschool offered a two-year-old program so we agreed to enroll Colton in that and thus a new personality was born: School Colton.

School Colton is the most well-behaved and obedient of all the Coltons. I observed this Colton once. He listened. He sat attentively with his hands folded on the desk in front of him. He raised his hand to speak. This new Colton was all business when it came to learning. I don't really like School Colton. He's too normal.

Two-year-old School Colton never missed a day of preschool. Three-year-old School Colton was a different story. Colton (the real one) started growing up which in turn made his other personalities grow up. School Colton was still the most obedient of all the Coltons but some days School Colton would "leave" class early. Some days School Colton didn't make it to class on time. Some days School Colton played hooky, while other days another Colton attended class disguised as School Colton until Mom and Dad were out of sight. Regardless of which Colton went to school that day, he always ran out of class happy as a clam.

Except this one time.

Colton sulks out of his classroom, shoulders slouched, feet dragging, a look of distress and exhaustion on his face.

COLTON: Ugh. Get me out of here.

CRYSTAL: What happened buddy?

COLTON: I. Don't. Want. To. Talk. About. It.

CRYSTAL: Is everything ok?

COLTON: Nope. No one gets me. Everything is not ok. I'm very very mad. This is the worst day ever.

Colton dramatically walks toward to the door, head hanging low.

CRYSTAL: Ok.

Colton's teacher Ms. D starts walking toward Crystal. Shit.

Ms. D starts to laugh. Shit?

MS. D: Is he telling you that he and I are "no longer on speaking terms?"

CRYSTAL: No. I was asking him about his day and he said, "I. Don't. Want. To. Talk. About. It."

MS. D: Welllll...he's really mad at me.

CRYSTAL: Colton. Come over here so we can talk to Ms. D about why you're not speaking to her.

COLTON: Fine.

CRYSTAL: Can you tell me why you're not talking to your teacher?

COLTON: She refused to call me Rhino Colton (He points to his hair). See?

It's important to mention that this morning Colton wanted his hair spiked in a mohawk, but he adjusted it into a single spike just above his forehead. A detail that would create a previously unknown personality, Rhino Colton.

CRYSTAL: Rhino Colton.

MS. D: Rhino Colton.

"OH NOW YOU CALL ME RHINO COLTON."

CRYSTAL: Buddy, we've gone over this. At school you have to be Colton. When you're not in school you can be whatever Colton you want to be.

MS. D: I love Rhino Colton. But I can't call you by another name in class. I have to call you Colton in class.

COLTON: Yeah, but what about my procedure?!

CRYSTAL: Procedure?

Stifling laughter, Ms. D smiles at Crystal.

COLTON: I went over this with Ms. D already. After school on Monday I had that procedure done to install my buttons.

CRYSTAL: Buttons? What buttons?

COLTON: THESE BUTTONS!

Colton drops to one knee, lifts his pant legs and pulls down his socks. He points to his left ankle bone.

COLTON: BAM! Push this one and I transform into a rhino.

He points to his right ankle bone.

COLTON: BAM! Push this one and I transform into a lion. I kept pushing my rhino button and no one would call me Rhino Colton. Meanwhile, I was clearly a rhino. I got mad and stomped around the class like the rhino I am. Ms. D said, "Colton, what are you doing?" And I told her, "Don't call me Colton." She said, "If I can't call you Colton then what am I supposed to call you?" And I said, "RHINO COLTON." Then the class laughed at me. And Ms. D and Ms. K laughed. And I got mad and told them, "If you can't call me Rhino Colton then don't talk to me any more."

CRYSTAL: Ok. Well, Rhino Colton you still need to be Colton in class. Is there anything you want to tell Ms. D?

COLTON: Sorry for getting mad.

MS. D: That's ok, Colton. High five?

COLTON: RHINO FIVE?

MS. D: Rhino five.

A Rhino five is the act headbutting someone's hand when they present their palm for a high five.

COLTON: Mom. Can we go now? I'm hungry.

Rhino Colton apparently worked up an appetite because he ate a cheeseburger, six nuggets, fries, an apple, two oranges, a bag of muffins and a chocolate milkshake for lunch.

Shit, I lost a kid!
Oh wait, never mind, found him...
Stuck behind toilet.

♡ A HAIKU FROM HUSBAND TO WIFE ♡

2016

chapter

14

ewton's first law of motion states that an object at rest stays at rest, and an object in motion stays in motion with the same speed and in the same direction unless acted upon by an unbalanced force.

Greyson is the object in motion.

He never stops. Ever. From 6:00 AM to 9:30 PM he moves. Even at a resting state he's still moving. G doesn't sleepwalk (at least not yet) but he does sleepwrestle his stuffed animals. One of them will inevitably end up on the floor while the other gets the bed. Despite G's restless and rambunctious nights, he always wakes up with a huge smile on his face.

Sometimes I wonder if his biological parents are actually Dennis the Menace and Taz. Maybe G was switched at birth and Dennis and Taz have our calm, quiet baby boy. But then I remember I was there, and that Taz and Dennis are cartoons incapable of bearing human children. Plus, there's the fact that Greyson looks exactly like Crystal and me.

Greyson's mischievous innocence is adorable and unrelenting. He's a blur of blonde hair moving through the house in one direction as arms, legs and miscellaneous extremities move in another. He means well but, good Lord, does he get into shit. Nothing is sacred.

Not even his beloved "FWAH FWAH B"—a crocheted blanket from my grandmother, his great-grandmother. Everything is a tool in his arsenal of hell-raising.

I love catching Greyson doing something he knows he shouldn't be doing. He knows the boundaries and if he's busted overstepping those boundaries he "falls asleep." He actually pretends to faint, like those goats on the internet. When you catch him doing something bad, he collapses onto the floor, closes his eyes and snores an exaggerated "HONK SHOO HONK SHOO." If you ask him what he's doing then he'll slowly open his eyes, yawn, stretch and respond with, "Go away I'm sleeping."

When he's not sleeping, Greyson is crazy fast.

He's an opportunist. He plays the sweet, innocent child card. Occupying himself with play. Smiling that adorable smile. Dialing up the cute factor to gain trust. Then you look away. He only needs four seconds to stop a parent's heart.

In four seconds he can cover sixty yards. [†]Experts say he's an aerodynamic child. It's some strange phenomenon that has to do with terminal velocity, the shape of his head and its forward/downward position that creates optimal thrust and drag. It's how rockets work, they say. I don't know what to think about that. I just think he's crazy. And fast.

People don't believe me when I say Greyson's really fucking fast. Someone always responds with, "Oh, but he's only one," or "He's a baby. How can he be that fast?"

G sees their questioning as a challenge and before Doubting Thomas can finish doubting G-SUS, he is gone.

Thankfully, there is one thing that can stop G dead in his tracks—music. It's an unbalanced force that's mesmerizing enough to slow him down so he can dance. He gets this from Taz. The only difference is Taz doesn't shout out voice commands like, "Google, EYEAHHHM

EYEUNNN MAHN!" or "Google, Hey Ho Let's Go!" when he wants to hear "Iron Man" or "Blitzkrieg Bop."

Crystal and I are so thankful for our Spotify Premium subscription. That $9.99/mo. (now with Hulu included) provides us with fifteen minutes of sanity a day. I don't know why the music soothes Greyson but I don't like to question it. It just works.

G has also somehow developed buttery-smooth dance moves, like unnaturally smooth for a baby or human of any age. His moves even change based on the genre. One minute he's popping shoulders like champagne bottles. The next his hands are keeping beats like they're fond memories. Then all of a sudden he's headbanging so hard that Cliff Burton probably sits up is his grave and says, "Fuck yeah, little man. Fuck yeah."

But, that's what happens when you're the third baby. You assimilate into the chaos. You absorb the chaos. You mold the chaos. You make the chaos your own. You have no other choice. Stand up. Stand out. Keep moving. Learn through observation and your siblings' encouraging fits of laughter while they watch in awe as you play bathtub hockey with a turd and a toothbrush.

Before Greyson I didn't think so much energy could fit into such a small body. And he certainly doesn't shy away from letting you know that he knows how to read a room. His eighteen-month check up came so fast we nearly forgot about it. But we didn't, and it happened to fall in one of those very rare windows of time when he was the only kid with Crystal.

That morning the two of them arrived at the doctor's. G was his normal energetic self, climbing into the reception window to chat up the staff in the office, exclaiming "OH WOW!" at the fish in the fish tank, dancing to the ever-so-faint music playing in the waiting room before getting called to the back.

Once Crystal and G were settled in the exam room, a nurse came in. She evaluated Greyson's height, weight, cranium circumference. All the usual. What's he eating? How's he sleeping? Yadda yadda yadda. The normal song and dance. Nothing out of the ordinary.

Up to that point Greyson had been laughing and practically scaling the walls because he knew his sweet little smile was enough for him to get away with murder. Then he read the nurse's lips as she mouthed *the* word to Mom.

"SHHHHHHHHHHHHHOTS."

Time slowed down. Panic set in. Greyson's demeanor changed. Shit, it's a trap! Mom sold me out. I gotta get outta here. The door. No. They're blocking the door. The window. Damn it. It's too high and the locks are an advanced grown-up technology that my inferior motor skills and tiny thumbs cannot comprehend. Maybe I'll fight my way out! Yeah! LET'S FIGHT!

BOOM. The shots were done. Quick and painless, at least for a moment. Then the sting set in (as it always does) and blood curdling screams echoed throughout the entire office. Crystal launched Spotify to play some JT and divert G's attention to the sunshine is his pocket and the good soul in his feet. His screams were soon replaced by those buttery-smooth dance moves. No more tears. That was easy.

Greyson high fived the nurse and waved buh-bye as she exited. The doctor would be in shortly.

Dressed in nothing more than a diaper, G spent the next fifteen minutes contorting his body so he could go spelunking into every single nook and cranny of the tiny room.

Knock knock! The doctor steps into the room and G climbs onto Crystal's lap.

GREYSON: Hi!

DOCTOR: Why hello, Mr. Greyson. How are you and Mom doing today?

GREYSON: GOOD.

DOCTOR: I heard you're a busy boy. Is that true?

GREYSON: YEAH!

Doctor looks at Crystal.

DOCTOR: Really?

CRYSTAL: Yeah...he's a busy one.

DOCTOR: Ok, Greyson. It seems like you're talkative.

Greyson enthusiastically nods his head.

GREYSON: YEAH!

DOCTOR: Can I ask you some questions today?

Greyson enthusiastically nods his head, again.

GREYSON: YEAH!

DOCTOR: What other words can you say?

GREYSON: Momma, Dadda, brothers, pup pup, meow meow...

DOCTOR: Wow. Very good!

Greyson applauds himself.

GREYSON: Yay!

DOCTOR: Ok, can I be your doctor today?

GREYSON: NNNNNOPE.

In one motion Greyson jumps off Crystal's lap, dekes around the doctor and makes it to the door. He opens the door and runs down the hall screaming.

GREYSON: NOOOOOOOOOOOOOOOOOO THANK YOU. BUB BYE!

The commotion is loud. He's drawn the attention and laughter of everyone. Crystal catches up to him at the door to the waiting room. His grand escape would have been a success if he wasn't laughing so hard that he couldn't fully stand on his tippy toes to reach the door knob. Crystal picks him up and football carries him back to the exam room as he desperately clings onto any object within arm's reach—nurses, desks, doors, filing cabinets, passing patients, etc.

GREYSON: NO OUCH NO OUCH NO OUCH NO OUCH NO OUCH!

Crystal plops him down on the table.

DOCTOR: You really are busy.

Greyson enthusiastically nods his head again.

GREYSON: YEAH!

I know Newton didn't have Greyson in mind when writing his first law of motion. Nor did he have any kids in mind when writing any of his theories. Newton didn't have kids. If he had kids then I'm sure his laws would have been written a little differently.

"A child at rest stays at rest until a parent steps on the creaking floorboard," or, "A child with a blanket over their head moves with the same speed and in the same direction unless acted upon by a wall."

Sounds fun, right?

It is fun.

Forever in motion fun.

---

†Ok, I have not consulted "experts" regarding Greyson's speed. And I have yet to subject him to any grueling speed tests. Doctors and professional looking people have stated "Wow! He is fast!" and while they're not rocket scientists I can only assume they're experts in their fields. So expert-ish people have said he's fast but I made that stuff up for shits and giggles.

2018

chapter

15

Imaginations are wonderful things. When used correctly they create worlds of play where the only limitations are the ones your mind creates. Cardboard boxes become transmogrifiers, wagons become spaceships and couch cushions are revered with the same majesty as a fifteenth-century fortress.

When used incorrectly, imaginations can creep the hell out of parents. Incorrectly probably isn't the right word though. Maybe unexpected? When imaginations are used in unexpected ways they can creep the hell out of parents.

Yeah, unexpected sounds better.

Paxton, Colton and Greyson use their imaginations to their fullest potentials. The majority of the time it seems like they can't shut them off. Especially at bedtime. Something always becomes something else, and that something else usually delays the process of going to sleep. Which is where this story started to develop.

Paxton and Colton share a room. If you recall, they insisted on bunk beds when they learned Mom had a baby in her tummy and eventually she would poop it out.

After a few weeks in the new room arrangement, we noticed Paxton waking up tired. He told us that Colton often stayed up playing and talking a lot throughout the night. When we asked Colton if that was true, he admitted it in a matter-of-fact manner like we were crazy for asking.

"Yeah, I do that. What do you expect me to do? Lay there and look at the wall? Borrrrring."

We talked to the two of them about it and expressed the need for a good night's sleep. Playtime has to end when the lights shut off or at least be at a very, very, very low volume. If they want to talk and laugh together as they fall asleep then that's ok, but once one of them is out, it's quiet time.

Paxton and Colton agreed and their sleep habits immediately improved. Though we would still hear Colton talking at all hours of the night.

Naturally we'd check on him any time we heard his voice. Most of the time he'd be sound asleep, snoring, mouth open with drool running down his cheek and onto his pillow. Some nights we would find him sitting up staring straight ahead with a blank look on his face, mumbling about something or laughing. Which was creepy as fuuuuuuuuuuuck.

Other nights we'd find him fighting crime. Those nights were the most frequent and would always start the same, with an audible "HAI YA!" followed by a flurry of karate chops, elbows, and roundhouse kicks—either on his bed or in the middle of their room.

Once at 1:30 AM, we woke to him yelling, "SLAAAAAAAAAAM DUNK!" followed by a thud, a giggle, and the pitter-patter of feet on the floor. Then, silence.

When I went in to check on him, Colton was sound asleep in bed. I noticed pillows and blankets on the floor, an overturned area rug, and a plastic basketball hoop lying on its side. A lone toy basketball slowly rolled across the floor, stopping at my feet.

Did my son just slam dunk a basketball in his sleep?

Colton had no recollection of that event but he did find it hilarious. He's becoming a sleepwalker. Yay!

Somehow Paxton sleeps through this stuff. Occasionally he will hear his brother doing something and chalks it up to Sleep Colton being Sleep Colton.

At some point, Colton started mentioning some character named Old Man Joesa while playing with his brothers and even alone. Crystal and I didn't think much of it at first since he would practically laugh his head off any time he mentioned the name Old Man Joesa.

I'm not talking a just chuckle, either. Colton would laugh a hearty belly laugh that we'd never heard before. His new laugh was hilarious and contagious which made the rest of the family laugh, and that in turn made Colton laugh harder. Eventually Old Man Joesa went from an occasional mention to a daily topic of playtime conversation.

Paxton started asking Colton what Old Man Joesa was doing right now or what he said, and the two of them would share a laugh and carry on playing.

Curiosity got the better of me after hearing them talk about this Old Man Joesa fellow so much. He's probably an imaginary friend or one of those multiple personalities that Colton cycles through, right?

ME: Hey Colton, who is this Old Man Joesa character?

"The dead guy in my room."

I nearly swallow my fucking tongue.

ME: The dead guy in your room?

COLTON: Yeah!

ME: Uh, who is this dead guy in your room?

COLTON: Old Man Joesa!

ME: Ooooook. Can you tell me more about him?

COLTON: He's this grumpy old man who doesn't use his manners. He's hilarious. He's always mad about something and we talk about why he's so grumpy.

ME: Um. Ok. Can tell me anything else about him?

COLTON: Yeah! He's super dead.

ME: And how do you know that he's dead?

COLTON: Uhhhhhhhhhhh, he's dead.

ME: He's dead? How did he die?

COLTON: He got shot in the eye by a bad guy.

ME: Shot in the eye? That sounds terrible. How'd that happen?

COLTON: I dunno. Some bad guy shot him in the eye and he died.

ME: And he died?

COLTON: Yup.

ME: What happened to the bad guy?

COLTON: He said the bad guy is in jail now.

ME: Sooooo, you two talk?

COLTON: Oh yeah.

ME: And when do you talk?

COLTON: At night.

ME: At night?

COLTON: That's what I said. At night. When everyone is sleeping.

I know their windows are locked but I check anyway.

ME: And he's grumpy?

COLTON: Oh yeah. Super grumpy.

ME: What does he do that makes him grumpy?

COLTON: This.

Colton makes a grumpy face.

ME: Is he mean?

COLTON: Sometimes. He doesn't use his manners and I tell him he needs to use his manners when talking because that's what you do when you talk to people.

ME: And what does he say to that?

COLTON: He gets grumpier.

ME: Does he bother you?

COLTON: Sometimes I just want to sleep and he will keep talking and being grumpy.

ME: And what do you do when he's grumpy and you're trying to sleep?

COLTON: I tell him, "Quit being a dickhead. I'm trying to sleep." Then I roll over and go to sleep.

ME: Then what?

COLTON: Then he shuts up and I go to sleep. But I haven't talked to him since I told him he was being a dickhead.

ME: Ok. Please stop saying dickhead.

COLTON: Well he was being one.

ME: I know. It's just not a nice thing to say to people.

COLTON: But he's a dead person.

ME: You said you haven't talked to him since you called him a dickhead? When was that?

COLTON: You're not suppose to say dickhead, Dad.

ME: ...When did you talk to him?

COLTON: I told you. A couple of days ago when I called him a D-word head. Then he left.

ME: What else can you tell me about Old Man Joesa?

COLTON: Well, he's dead. And he's grumpy. He never uses his manners. His wife's name is Lacey and she is dead, too. They're both super dead.

ME: He has a wife?

COLTON: Had a wife, yeah, but she's dead too.

ME: How do you know he had a wife?

COLTON: He said, "My wife died."

ME: What does he look like?

COLTON: He wears a brown shirt and black shoes and has a blue walking stick.

ME: Ok.

COLTON: And he's from Japan.

ME: Where?

COLTON: JA-PAN.

We've never talked about Japan. As far as I know Colton knows nothing about Japan and shouldn't know anything since world geography is a little beyond the three-year-old preschool curriculum.

ME: Japan. Interesting.

COLTON: Yeah, it's like really far away. And he likes rabbits.

ME: Rabbits? Ok, Donnie Darko.

COLTON: His name isn't Donnie, Dad. His name is Old Man Joesa and he's dead.

I can't say with definitive proof that Old Man Joesa is a wayward spirit. Maybe he is? Or maybe he's an imaginary friend with an incredibly complicated and creative backstory? Either way I think it's pretty cool. After all, "The creative adult is the child who survived after the world tried killing them."

If that's true then I wonder what killed Old Man Joesa.

"The creative adult is the child who survived after the world tried killing them, making them grown up. The creative adult is the child who survived the blandness of schooling, the unhelpful words of bad teachers, and the nay-saying ways of the world. The creative adult is in essence simply that, a child." - **Julian F. Fleron**

No one wins WHO can be the Quietest.

Dan's Dadvice

2017

chapter 16

hree-Year-Old School Colton is dead. Gonzo. Fini. No more. I kinda expected that since Two-Year-Old School Colton was eventually replaced/upgraded. But Two-Year-Old School Colton went quietly. Poof. He faded into the ether like a fart in church. Three-Year-Old School Colton, on the other hand, did not go that easily.

Colton is wise beyond his years. Too wise for a three-year-old. Hell, half of the time he's too wise for a thirty-three-year-old. If it wasn't for the whole talking to the dead guy in his room thing then I'd say he has life figured out. Then again, maybe the dead guy isn't a hurdle since he seems to have exorcised him by calling him dickhead before turning over and going to sleep.

So maybe three-year-old preschool was a bit below him? That's not a jab at his teachers. They were great. Colton loved them. But he reached a point where he wasn't challenged anymore. Honestly, I have a feeling that's going to be a recurring theme with School Colton's education. I wouldn't be surprised if he rocked a straight 2.0 GPA out of sheer boredom and/or defiance. If the kid isn't challenged then he completely checks out.

School Colton will always be an evolving enigma. The last day of three-year-old preschool showed that.

The last day of preschool is basically a funfest. Colton's school hosts a carnival with a bunch of activity stations—bounce houses, ice cream, bubble painting, obstacle courses, etc. The students burn off energy. The teachers sigh in relief. The parents get to experience the chaos of twenty-some three-year-olds in one room together.

Colton had the same teachers for two and three-year-old preschool—Ms. D and Ms. K.

Ms. D and Ms. K grew to know Colton well. They learned his quirks and mannerisms and understood that 99% of the time he's unpredictable. Naturally at the end of the year, teachers can feel a tinge of sadness watching their students grow up and move on. So it wasn't surprising that Ms. D and Ms. K wanted to take a moment to say their goodbyes and wish their pupils the best. Or as Colton would describe it, "They wanted to get all sappy and shit."

Colton is not a "sappy and shit" kinda kid. I rarely get a hug out of him, though he does tell Crystal, Paxton, Greyson and me, "I love you and my entire family!" constantly, so that's nice.

His emotional side is about as soft as a grizzled old man who's seen heinous sights. His idea of affection is chopping your head off. Colton leans in like he wants to whisper something endearing in your ear. This tricks the recipient into leaning closer. When your head is right next to his, Colton will slowly raise and extend one hand. He'll rest that hand on your shoulder and look you straight in the eye. He'll take a small breath and yell, "CHOP YOUR HEAD OFF!" as his hand quickly slides across the base of your neck. Getting your head chopped off by Colton is high praise. It means he loves you.

So, the last day carnival came to an end. Ms. D and Ms. K were getting all sappy and shit and wanted to take a moment with each student before they rode off into the summer. Colton was ready to leave and had visions of ice cream and milkshakes twerking in his head. But then Ms. D and Ms. K stopped him to say goodbye and asked for the impossible—end of the year hugs.

I *thought* I knew how this would end. But I wasn't expecting to witness the death of Three-Year-Old School Colton in the form of a phoenix combusting into flames and emerging from the ash as Four-Year-Old School Colton

The word "hug" hung in the atmosphere, stopping Colton dead in his tracks. He turned to look back at his teachers, stone-faced.

Shit.

Yup. This is...wait, he's not moving. He's standing there. Just staring. He's thinking. This is good. He's processing the correct emotional response. We talked about this. Hallelujah, he was listening! Yes! He's actually going to hug them. Crisis avoided! Thank God!

Colton walks toward his teachers. He takes a deep breath and stands between Ms. K and Ms. D.

He turns toward Ms. K and assumes a ninja stance.

COLTON: CHOP YOUR ARM OFF! CHOP THIS ARM OFF, TOO!

*THWAC**KKKKK***

Oh sweet baby Jesus all swaddled up in the manger.

He just slapped his teacher on the ass.[†]

The room went silent.

All eyes turned to Colton as he turned to Ms. D.

He calmly leans toward his other teacher.

COLTON: CHOP YOUR HEAD OFF!

Colton makes a chopping motion over her heck and marches toward the door. He stops and turns to look at his teachers and classmates one last time.

He raises both hands high into the air and throws up double peace signs.

"SAYONARA SUCKERS! I'M IN MS. LALA'S CLASS NOW!"

Thank God he didn't toss up double traffic fingers. That would have been awkward.

†To clarify the "slap" was like a "good job" slap between teammates not, like a shorty is thicc and Daddy like slap. Regardless, I was not too thrilled with the slap. The head and arm chopping was totally fine. The "slap" warranted another conversation about personal space and what is considered an appropriate gesture of gratitude.

Baby talk is dumb.

Talk to your baby like a person. Carry on conversations with them, even if they don't respond.
They know what you're saying and when they begin to talk they'll build off your vocabulary.

Dan's DADVICE

2017

chapter

17

stala ctites
&
stala GMiTeS

ere's a terrible riddle I just made up:

I am both a spaceship and a cave.
I have a top and a bottom.
I comfort and cause fights.

What am I?

drrrrrrrrrrrrumroll please

I AM A BUNK BED and I've been making sleep an adventure since 2800 B.C. or something like that.

Ahhhh, bunk beds. The king of twin beds. Le château du sommeil. An amazing double-decker beacon of childhood freedom. They're like sleeping in a fort every single night. My brother and I had them growing up, so when Paxton and Colton asked for bunk beds the nostalgia hit me right in the feels like a Sock'em Bopper to the nose. Flashbacks of late night giggle-fests and "Hey...are you awake?" filled my head. What could possibly go wrong with bunk beds?!?!

Bunk beds are awesome 99.8% of the time. But you gotta watch out for that other .02%. It comes out of nowhere and I learned that firsthand within two years of The Big Bro Bunk Suite.

Cue flashback sequence.

Christmas Eve 2017. Our family of five is preparing for a fun holiday break together. The boys are conjuring up ways to capture

Santa. Like really planning to catch Santa. One of their plans even involved using baby Greyson as bait. Ingenious!

I joined in on the scheming until Colton had a change of heart. He didn't want to ruin Christmas morning for all the other kids if they captured Santa, so he and Paxton agreed to stop talking about it before word got back to the big guy.

We do have a very talkative Elf on the Shelf—Dillard Von Chippersteen. He is watching you. He's always watching. Gotta love the most adorable police state ever!

I noticed a visible shift in Colton's demeanor once they stopped planning the capture. He sat next to me on the couch and told me his stomach hurt. His head was hot. He climbed onto my lap and I covered us with a blanket. He started to doze off.

I love these moments. They don't happen often but when they do they're incredible. Colton is almost out of this stage because it's not "cool" and "he's not a baby", so unfortunately cuddle time with him is coming to an end. It sucks. They don't stay little for long.

Colton looked up at me. His eyes opened and he looked angelic. Typically in these moments he will say something sweet like, "I love you," or "thanks for being my dad," or "I'm so happy to have you in my life."

So when he opened his mouth I expected my heart to melt. But instead of words, projectile vomit spewed all over me, the couch and the living room rug.

He opened his mouth again. "Sorry Da—" and out came more puke.

"It's ok, buddy," I reassured him as I picked him up and ran to the bathroom. A trail of vomit followed us.

This scenario played on repeat over the next few days. Not exactly the gift I was hoping for that holiday.

Then Crystal got it.

Greyson got it.

And Paxton got it, sometime between Christmas Eve and New Year's Eve.

Around 2:00 AM muffled noises followed by a low, "Mommmmmm" woke Crystal and I up.

We ran into The Big Bro Bunk Suite and turned on the light. Paxton was sitting up on the top bunk covered in vomit. I still can't believe how much barf came out of him. His pajamas were covered. The top bunk was covered. The walls, the ceiling, the sheets, comforter and pillows were all covered in a brown sludgey mixture of what looked like chocolate milk and Jet-Puffed Marshmallow Creme.

I lowered Paxton out of bed and helped him into a warm shower. After I carefully corralled the mess formerly known as the top bunk, I stopped to sit down on Colton's bed below. I gathered my thoughts and calmed my stomach, watching him sleep for a few minutes. I adjusted his blankets around him so I knew he was tucked in and comfortable.

Miraculously, Colton slept through Paxton barfing all over the top bunk. It was the first time in a few days he was actually sleeping soundly. I was thankful for that. He wasn't throwing up and the color was coming back in his face. He looked angelic, like a cute little angel baby lying there (Colton is going to be so mad when he reads this later in life).

I stood up to finish cleaning the mess and it hit me. Literally. Something hit me. What the hell was this wet slop that just landed on my shoulder? Eww. I felt it sliding down my back.

I looked up and saw it. Stalactites of vomit. Long stringy strands of that brown sludgey chocolate milk Jet-Puffed mixture hanging from the underside of the mattress.

How the fuck did Paxton manage to barf *there*? How do I clean it up? Do I burn the mattress? When will this stop?!

I looked back at Colton. He was sitting straight up. His eyes were wide, and his movements were trance-like. I didn't hear him wake up.

We locked eyes.

"Dad, I think I'm gonna pu—"

Round two. Ding. Ding. A steady flow of that brown sludgey mixture cascaded over blankets, stuffed animals and myself. Every stalactite needs a stalagmite and this cave of comfort just experienced 150,000 years of rock formation in a matter of minutes.

I got Colton out of bed and into a shower.

When I returned to the Big Bro Bunk Suite to assess the damage, I realized that bunk beds do in fact have a downside. And that downside smells terrible. I cleaned up the mess and gagged until I puked a bit myself. But at least I made it to the trash can.

Anarchy is Christmas Morning without Coffee.

Dan's DADVICE

Eggplant emoji

Taco winky face and peach

Hey! Are we sexting?!

♡ A HAIKU FROM HUSBAND TO WIFE ♡

2017

chapter

18

uck the kid leash! I hate those things. I never understood them. WHY? Why do parents strap those things to their kid to like he or she is some sort of canine-human hybrid trained to walk on two legs, or at the very least lie down in protest to be dragged through the zoo? Get up, you're going to miss the snow leopard, dummy.

It screams lazy parent. Look! I can't be bothered to watch my kid or transport them safely, so I'll strap an adorable monkey to their back and remove the proverbial one from mine.

I've wanted to pet those kids. I've wanted to ask them to sit, stay, shake, roll over, play dead and then reward them with scratches behind the ear. They deserve a treat, right?

If I was that kid then I'd resent my parents for doing that to me, I thought. How humiliating, I thought. How absolutely embarrassing for both parent and child, I thought. I would never put a leash on Paxton. I would never put a leash on Colton. I would never put a leash on Greyson, I thought.

I thought wrong.

I owe every parent or guardian I ever judged an apology. I get it now. You have a Greyson. An object forever in motion. You now have my sympathy. I want to sit down and cry with you.

The leash conversation was hands down the hardest parenting talk to date. We'd just finished planning our first family vacation to the beach.

Crystal looked at me with defeat in here eyes. "Soooo, G needs a—"

"A leash. I know," I sighed.

Damn it.

We had a good run. We'd managed to bring up two toddlers without having to call for reinforcements. But Crystal was right. Greyson needed a leash. He needed to be restrained for his safety, and our sanity.

Greyson broke into a Claire's once. That teen/tween store in the mall that sells earrings and stuff. Thankfully most states won't prosecute an eighteen-month-old for unlawful entry. But Mom and Dad will with a ten dollar purchase from Amazon.

Crystal stopped by the mall to let G burn some energy after dropping School Colton off at class. It was early, before the stores opened, and the only other folks in the mall were the elderly walkers.

All the gates were closed with the exception of Claire's. The Claire's gate was propped open about eight inches. Greyson saw this well before Mom did.

He performed his cute, well-rehearsed act. He walked ahead of Mom a few steps, occasionally glancing over his shoulder to smile. He dialed up the adorable by greeting all the geriatric couples walking the mall with an enthusiastic "Hi!" and a wave.

"Awwww he's so sweet," they said. "How cute!" they said.

His plan was working.

G hears some music.

G stops to dance.

Mom stops to tie her shoe.

G smiles at Mom.

Mom smiles at G.

Crap. G's running.

Now Mom is running.

G's running toward Claire's.

Mom is a half-step behind G.

G slides on his stomach and slips right under the gate.

G is inside the store.

Mom is not inside the store.

G waves at Mom.

G sticks out tongue.

G blows raspberries.

G hears music again.

G stops to dance again.

Mom squeezes under the gate.

G laughs.

G runs again.

Mom is in the store now.

Mom is not happy.

G runs around the merchandise desperately trying to avoid capture.

"Does anyone work here?!"

Mom catches G.

Mom squeezes under the gate dragging G in one hand.

G yells things like, "NO!" "OW!" and "HELP!"

Claire's employee emerges from back of store.

Claire's employee sees Mom and G stuck under gate.

Claire's employee says nothing.

Claire's employee does nothing.

Mom makes it under gate with G in hand.

Mom thanks Claire's employee for "opening" the gate.

G gets a leash for beach.

Greyson is the reason we fenced in our backyard. Our yard is not a small yard, just under an acre, so he had many escape routes. He enjoyed running toward the street. He enjoyed running into the woods. He enjoyed running into the neighbors yard five houses away.

He gave us no choice.

The day I finished the last panel on the fence Greyson ugly cried, hard. But he performed his normal routine first. He played the cute card, smiling and waving like a precious little angel. He even blew us kisses. Oh boy was he hamming it the fuck up.

We intentionally looked away because we knew he would run. And run he did.

He ran toward the edge of the yard. There he discovered the previously open fence panel was now closed. He walked a few feet to his left. Nope. Fence. He ran to his right. Nope. Fence. He turned and crossed the yard in a panic only to find fence on that side, too. He ran toward the side yard. Fence! He ran to the other side of the house. Fence, again. He frantically ran from escape route to escape route. Fence, fence and more fence.

G began screaming.

"OH NO. I. CAN'T. GO! MOMMA! I CAN'T GO! I CAN'T GO!"

G collapsed on the ground in a tantrum. He held his breath. He changed colors. He yelled and flopped around like a fish out of water. And for the first time in eighteen months I sat down in the backyard and enjoyed an ice cold piña colada with my beautiful wife.

That's what success tastes like.

Memorized the list.
Grocery shopping like a boss!
Forgot milk...again.

♡ A HAIKU FROM HUSBAND TO WIFE ♡

Kids bump their heads.

If a bump bubbles out that's probably an ok bump.
If a bump bubbles in that's definitely a bad bump.

Dan's
DADVICE

2015

chapter

19

Do you remember your first glass of chocolate milk? What a truly life changing moment. That crisp, cold, liquid chocolate tantalizing ten thousand taste buds with a gentle caress as it trickles into your tummy. It's the closest you can get to heaven without actually going to heaven.

Normal milk? Pssh. Please. You might as well drink khakis. All aboard the chocolate train. Next stop, your mouth. Now add a smidge of heat, some marshmallows and oh momma you just one-upped yourself. Hot chocolate! Sweet Buddha, we've reached nirvana.

But like any good thing, kids find a way to destroy it. It's true. They have a knack for making the mundane chaotic. Not just any chaotic but holy fucking shit how in the h-e-double-hockey-sticks is this even *possible* kind of chaotic.

Take childbirth for instance. Movies and TV shows make it seem so calm and photogenic. It is magical, but those calm and photogenic moments come after crowning. And that's just a toe in the water moment of parenting. Kids only get crazier from then on.

Heads up, if the thought of crowning makes you squeamish then you probably won't like this story. No, this story doesn't involve childbirth. But it may scare off some of the readers who are considering having kids.

The year is 2015. It was an early spring afternoon. March 7th, to be exact. Colton was a chunky little gremlin bouncing around a living room filled with new toys after his first birthday party. Paxton was two and was also really excited, since his brother's new toys were basically his new toys by association.

The afternoon had been peaceful. Crystal was preparing for her parents to come over for dinner later, while I motherfucked some overly-complicated child's plaything into submission to finish building it. You could feel the happiness in the air.

PAXTON: Momma. Hot choc-it please.

CRYSTAL: Great job using your words and your manners, buddy. High five.

PAXTON: I love hot choc-it. Can I have now?

CRYSTAL: Yeah bud, but I need to make it first.

PAXTON: Can I make?

CRYSTAL: Yeah, you can help me. Here, I'll give you a job.

PAXTON: Ok Momma. Hot choc-it. Hot choc-it. Hot choc-it.

Crystal sits Paxton next to her on the kitchen counter. Paxton is dancing as he sings his hot chocolate song. Crystal joins in on the song and dance.

CRYSTAL: Packie, can you hold this cup for me?

PAXTON: Hot choc-it. Hot choc-it. Hot choc-it.

CRYSTAL: Hot choc-it. Hot choc-it. Hot choc-it.

Crystal dances to the pantry to grab the Swiss Miss and marshmallows.

PAXTON: Hot choc-it. Hot choc-it. Hot choc-it.

CRYSTAL: Hot choc-it. Hot choc-it. Hot choc-it.

Crystal sets the Swiss Miss and marshmallows next to Paxton on the counter and grabs milk from the fridge.

PAXTON: (Screaming because why not?) I LOVE HOT CHOC-IT!

CRYSTAL: Paxton, hold this cup for me ok?

PAXTON: Yes, Momma.

Crystal pours the milk. It didn't spill. He actually held the cup!

CRYSTAL: Great job, Pax!

Crystal turns to put the milk away. Paxton knocks the cup of milk off the counter.

PAXTON: Oh no, my hot choc-it!

CRYSTAL: That's ok. It's just milk. I'll make a new one.

PAXTON: (Sad whimper) Hot choc-it. (Screams again because— kid) I LOVE HOT CHOC-IT!

Crystal bends down to clean up the spill.

PAXTON: I WANT HOT CHOC-IT!

Paxton picks up the Swiss Miss packet and begins to shake it in front of him. Crystal doesn't know he's waving the packet like a maniac as the temper tantrum starts.

PAXTON: I WANT HOT CHOC-IT! MOM! MOM! MOM! MOM! MOM! MOM! MOM! MOM! MOM! MOM! MOM! HOT CHOC-IT!

Crystal stands up to look at him and that's when I hear it. The horrible shriek to end all horrible shrieks.

Author's note: I honestly don't know how to describe the sound. If I had to spell it and read it back to you then I would just mash my face into my keyboard and shout the random assembly of characters in one long exhale of unimaginable pain. So that's what I'm going to do.

"FUGSBONHAMIERASUNKFR UTYFGJJGFDVOBYUHESUIN PGMHTPHHHHNUOHJESUS WHYGODFFAHHHHHHHHK"

Crystal runs down the hall to the bathroom. She's crying.

PAXTON: Uh-oh.

Asshole Dan thinks Crystal stubbed her toe and is overreacting.

CRYSTAL: DAN! DAN! I need you in the bathroom right now!

ME: Oook. I'll be right there.

I walk into the kitchen to get Paxton down off the counter. He's clutching his Swiss Miss packet, terrified.

CRYSTAL: DAN! Where are you?

ME: I'm coming. I was getting Pax off the counter.

Crystal's holding her left eye with one hand. Tears are running down that cheek.

CRYSTAL: I feel a flap. Oh God.

ME: A flap?

CRYSTAL: Yes. A fucking flap.

ME: A flap? Where?

CRYSTAL: On my eyeball. There's a flap on my eyeball. I can feel it. It's fucking flapping.

ME: What happened?

CRYSTAL: Really?! Did you not hear me scream?

ME: Oh, I did. But what happened?

CRYSTAL: He spilled his milk and when I stood up after cleaning it up he was yelling, "HOT CHOC-IT HOT CHOC-IT," and waving that stupid Swiss Miss packet around like an idiot and he sliced my goddamn eye with it, Dan.

ME: He sliced your eye?

CRYSTAL: Yeah. My eye. And now there's a flap.

ME: Let me see. How could there be a—

I hold her head steady and get close to her face. Crystal removes her hand and slowly opens her eye. I see a straight vertical line directly over her pupil, opening up into a perfectly peeled flap revealing parts of my wife that I never wanted to see or imagined seeing.

ME: FLAP! Holy shit it's a flap! Oh fuck! IT'S A FLAP!

CRYSTAL: I TOLD YOU THERE WAS A FLAP! I COULD FEEL IT. OH GOD I CAN SEE IT. THE FLAP IS A LINE. I SEE A LINE AND FEEL A FLAP.

ME: Ok. Uhhhh, close your eye and hold your hand over it so it doesn't...flap. Let me grab my phone and figure out what to do.

CRYSTAL: Ok.

I step away to frantically WebMD this. The search results were not pretty.

I call Crystal's parents and let them know that dinner is postponed until later tonight and they need to watch the kids while I take her to the ER. I call the ER. They tell me to take her to the optometrist. I call the optometrist. They tell me to get her to them immediately.

Paxton tiptoes down the hallway.

PAXTON: Mommy. Are you ok?

CRYSTAL: I dunno, buddy.

PAXTON: I'm sorry.

CRYSTAL: You're ok, Pax.

He holds up the Swiss Miss.

PAXTON: Hot choc-it, please?

CRYSTAL: Haha. Go sit on the couch, please.

ME: He really wants that hot choc-it, huh?

CRYSTAL: Yup.

The optometrist ended up being the right call. She took a look at Crystal's eye and assured us that while it was incredibly painful and uncomfortable, the human eye heals really fast. Crystal's vision would be fine; the Swiss Miss didn't cut deep enough to damage anything severely. Crystal would just have to rock an eye patch for at least a week and apply medicated drops twice a day.

You know she made that eye patch look damn sexy.

And yes, Paxton got his hot choc-it when we got home. He even helped Mom make it after he put on his own pirate eye patch so they could match.

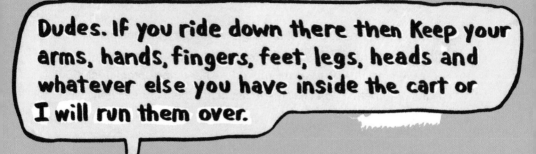

Eat the Cookies!

If you want a cookie and find the remaining cookies are equal to or less than the number of kids you have then eat the remaining cookies. Don't tell them. Don't let them hear you. Just eat the cookies, quietly. This also applies to ice cream, candy and cereal.

Dan's
DADVICE

2019

chapter

20

IF YOU GIVE
a TWO-YEAR-OLD
APPLE JUICE

I f You Give a Two-Year-Old Apple Juice sounds more like a Laura Numeroff children's book than a series of events that unfolded in our home. This story is not a Laura Numeroff children's book. Trust me. We have (almost) all of her books. They're some of our favorite bedtime stories. If You Give a Two-Year-Old Apple Juice would be a shitty bedtime story anyway.

Three things you need to know about this story. First, it started with apple juice. Obviously. Second *SPOILER ALERT* it ends in stitches. Third, this story is the perfect example of how kids can make even the most mundane things chaotic.

Paxton, Colton and Greyson LOVE apple juice. I love it too. But for some reason too much of it gives us diarrhea. Maybe that's normal? Maybe it's hereditary? Kids inherit their parents weird quirks so the idea of inheriting food sensitivities and subpar digestive enzymes is not a far-fetched concept.

All I know is that apple juice gives me the squirts, but I drink it anyway because it's delicious and refreshing. I just try to limit my consumption to a glass or two so I don't have one of those accidents my wife and kids tease me about.

The boys on the other hand, haven't learned their apple juice limit.

It was a normal Saturday afternoon. We spent some time visiting my grandma, the boys' Great Grandma. Greyson drank apple juice, ate a bunch of stuff and played. I lost track of how many cups of apple juice he drank and didn't think to keep count since I was more focused on multi-generational family bonding. It was a pleasantly uneventful afternoon.

When the visit was over we drove back home and retired to the basement for playtime, endless snacking and fort building. Paxton and Colton played video games in their fort as Greyson pinballed around the room. Crystal and I curled up on the couch and decided to catch up on season two of *Making a Murderer*. We watched two and a half episodes with limited interruptions.

Just as we neared the end of the first episode, a horrid smell wafted through the basement. It was coming from Greyson. He pooped. No big deal. We were surprised that was only our first interruption.

I paused the show so Crystal could change him. When he was ready to go, he ran off back to do his pinball thing. We resumed and got all the way to the credits.

We started the second episode. PAUSE. The boys wanted something to eat. Interruption number two. They were undecided at first. After a few minutes of back and forth questioning, we all agreed on the Snack Box and refills of their drinks.

Paxton and Colton asked for water. Greyson asked for apple juice. Sure. Whatever. Snack Box and refills for everyone. I want to know if Dassey makes bond, so let's do this quick! The boys were content as they happily ate, played and drank. UNPAUSE.

We finished the second episode.

Before starting a third consecutive episode, I should make sure everyone was good on snacks and drinks. Greyson asked for apple juice, again, but I knew he had enough for one day. Any more and he'd be crapping out of his pants and up his back. No thank you. Here's your water, Danger Baby.

Danger Baby was mad. Danger Baby reluctantly took the water from my hand and sulked back to the fort.

Crystal and I were pumped. We were actually watching a show together with limited interruptions! I couldn't believe it. We started the third episode.

Twenty-seven minutes into the third consecutive episode the third and final interruption interrupted us.

Our adorable littlest boy climbed over the back of the couch. He poked his head in between Crystal and I and rolled onto my lap. He looked up at us and smiled that sweet innocent smile that only Danger Baby can smile when he's trying to hide something.

"I love you Dada. I love you Momma," he said.

"Awww. We love you too Greyson," we answered in unison.

But the horrid smell was back. The same smell from earlier. Only worse. It was that first smell, but only if that smell was left to ferment in the blistering sun for hours.

"Oh God! You pooped again?" I asked.

"YEAH!" G said.

It was my turn to change him. PAUSE. I picked G up and turned him around so he could "fly" to the changing station.

"OH GOD! HE HAD TOO MUCH APPLE JUICE!" I shouted. "It's up his back. To his shoulder blades. Uhhh...check the couch. Check everywhere he was playing. I'm taking him upstairs to get cleaned up."

"I pooped big, Dada," he giggled.

Miraculously, the poop only got on Greyson.

That third and final interruption was the big one. It snapped us back to reality. No more binge watching. That was a nice one hundred and forty-nine minute vacation. Time to parent again.

I bathed Greyson as Crystal whipped up dinner. Grilled cheese was on the menu and was slowly making its way into our five or six basic food groups.

Greyson loves playing in the bathtub. Before each bath he hand-selects his "bath" toys which usually are not bath toys. His bath time excitement level correlates to the number of toys he brings into the tub. That night he was really excited so he loaded the tub with every Mr. Potato Head character and Mr. Potato Head accessory in the house.

I should mention we have nine different Mr. Potato Heads and buckets of all their accessories. Keep 'em coming Playskool.

At the thirty-one minute mark I began to plead with him to get out of the tub. I tried to bribe him. I made it seem like something really exciting was happening somewhere that wasn't the bathtub. But Greyson wasn't buying what I was selling.

Oh well. At least the water was still nice and warm. Nothing was going to pry him out of the tub until he was ready.

"Boys, your grilled cheeses are done," Crystal called from the dining room.

Greyson stood up, climbed out of the tub and yelled, "GRILLED CHEESE!"

He ran out of the bathroom. I couldn't catch him, he was naked and wet. Best to just let him be naked and wet for a few minutes.

Greyson streaked straight into the dining room, where Paxton and

Colton were sitting at the table. They laughed, which encouraged G to get crazier. He danced in circles. He stopped. He faced his brothers, tossed his hands over his head and shook his hips to and fro.

"PEE PEE! PEE PEE!" he screamed.

Paxton and Colton laughed harder. G laughed harder.

I managed to toss a towel around G. He followed me back to the bathroom where I dried him off. He started to dance again. As I turned away for just a second to drain the bath, my peripheral vision caught G doing a handstand on the edge of the tub.

I am constantly yelling at the boys, "DON'T PLAY, SIT, STAND, JUMP, DANCE, ETCETERA ON THE EDGE OF THE TUB! YOU'RE GOING TO FALL AND GET HURT!"

Doesn't matter. They still do it. Every other time before this I managed to catch them before they fell. But on that day my dad reflexes were not fast enough.

I knew what was about to happen. I quickly turned around and reached for his leg. I missed.

Greyson's left hand slipped into the tub. His right hand slipped out of the tub. Boom. He fell chin first onto the side of the bathtub, hard enough to shake the room.

G let out a weird grunt as he bounced onto the bathroom floor.

I immediately picked him up. Greyson cried and held his chin. I sat down on the edge of the tub and positioned G on my lap. I held his hand and pressed his head against my chest in an effort to calm him down. I know that hurt.

His crying slowed.

I tilted his head back to look at his chin.

"Holy shit!" I said. "We have to go to the ER right now! This is gonna need stitches!"

But Greyson wasn't crying anymore. He cried a very short cry and shook it off. In fact, he rolled his eyes at my reaction.

I'm pretty sure he has Congenital Insensitivity to Pain. That's a real thing. Google it. It's like the pain receptors never developed in the womb. How else could he headbutt walls in defiance for being told not to eat toilet paper? He doesn't react to pain. One time Crystal accidentally slammed his hand in the car door and the door latched shut. He just looked at her like, "dafuq Mom?" before opening the door, pulling his hand out and skampering off. He is Danger Baby, the most dangerous baby to ever live.

So, I rushed Danger Baby out to the living room. Crystal asked him what happened. G tilted his back and pointed to his chin.

"Momma. I fell and hit chin on tub," his chin said, as the gash was opening and closing as G spoke. It wasn't bleeding, yet. But fuck was it deep.

Apparently diarrhea up the back was not the final interruption. This was.

Crystal and I put our heads together and quickly figured out what to do. We are a magnificent team!

That's a lie, she figured it out. I just paced the living room quietly muttering obscenities to myself a she calmly talked me through what needed to happen.

Greyson's chin finally started to bleed. He either didn't care or didn't notice. He was smiling and wanted to play. I managed to dress him so Crystal could take him to the emergency room.

That's another lie, Crystal dressed him. I was too busy panicking to figure out how shirts work.

Colton and Paxton were worried. They saw Greyson's chin and the blood and knew he was hurt, even though he didn't outwardly show any signs of pain or discomfort.

Crystal walked us through the plan. Dad, Paxton and Colton would stay home and finish their grilled cheese sandwiches while she and G would go for a quick car ride to the hospital so a nice doctor could fix his chin with a couple of stitches.

"DOCTOR? NO DOCTOR, MOMMA!" Greyson protested, stomping his foot

Somehow Crystal persuaded Greyson to go with her and before I knew it he was dancing and waving on his way out the door. I settled in at the table with the older two and reassured them that Greyson would be ok.

Meanwhile, Greyson was loving his adventure to the ER. He saw it as an opportunity to show off and ham it up from the moment he walked in.

NURSE: Hello. What can I help you with?

" **Are you a doctor?** " Greyson said.

The nurse laughs.

NURSE: No, I am not a doctor, sweetie.

GREYSON: Ok. I fell. Hit my chin. See.

G tilts his head back and points to his chin.

NURSE: Oh my. Yes, you did. And you're not even crying. You must be tough.

CRYSTAL: Yeah, he doesn't feel pain.

The nurse checks Crystal and Greyson into the emergency room.

NURSE: Can I put this wristband on you so the doctor will see you, Greyson?

GREYSON: Nope. Bye.

Before Crystal can react he jumps off her lap and sprints toward the exit.

He dekes around some chairs in the lobby.

He slides across the floor.

Crystal is chasing after him.

This is Claire's all over again but now he's faster. And bleeding.

G sees the large double doors leading to the ER. He changes direction. He makes a beeline for them.

The doors open and he squeezes through them.

Crystal grabs his hoodie.

G has been caught. He laughs and yells.

GREYSON: NO DOCTORS. NO DOCTORS.

Crystal wears G's wristband.

NURSE: Dude! YOU ARE FAST!

CRYSTAL: Yeah. This is why you're getting stitches tonight, isn't it?

GREYSON: YEAH!

The nurse instructs Crystal and Greyson to follow a second nurse to get his weight and a few other things checked out before they can be admitted into a room. They follow Nurse 2 through a set of doors into a small room.

NURSE 2: Hi Greyson.

" Hi. Are you a doctor? "

Nurse 2 laughs.

NURSE 2: No, I am not a doctor. I'm a nurse. I'm here to help you with your boo boo. Is that ok?

GREYSON: YEAH!

NURSE 2: Thank you. Can you step on this scale so I can weigh you before the doctor sees you?

Greyson walks toward the scale. He stops to check it out. He looks at the nurse then looks back at Mom.

GREYSON: Nope. Bye. NO DOCTORS!

Greyson is running, again. This time through the emergency room. He runs by more nurses, doctors and patients in their rooms. He is laughing and yelling. He is loud. He is drawing A LOT of attention.

GREYSON: NO DOCTORS! NO DOCTORS!

Crystal chases after Greyson.

Everyone sees them. Laughter fills the emergency room.

GREYSON: Try and catch me, Mom. TRY AND CATCH ME!

Crystal finally snags him and football carries him back to Nurse 2's room.

NURSE 2: Mom. You are fast and calm. I wish more parents were like you. Greyson, you on the other hand...are a very, very fast kid. Your poor mom. Bless her heart.

GREYSON: YEAH!

Crystal and Greyson get admitted into a room. The hallways are buzzing with talk about "that ridiculously fast child who was running through the hallways laughing and yelling NO DOCTORS."

A few minutes pass and the doctor comes in to talk to Crystal and Greyson.

Greyson is sitting on Crystal's lap watching YouTube on her phone.

DOCTOR: You must be Greyson.

" **Yup. Are you a doctor?** "

DOCTOR: I am a doctor!

Greyson drops Crystal's phone and jumps off her lap.

GREYSON: Mom, I said NO DOCTORS. MOM. NO! DOCTORS!

G tries to run, again. Mom was prepared this time. Mom wins.

The doctor steps out for a minute and returns with reinforcements, new nurses.

Crystal bear-hugs Greyson and holds his head still.

The nurses aid in restraining Greyson before he can Hulk out.

The doctor begins stitching Greyson's chin.

GREYSON: NO DOCTORS! GO AWAY! GO AWAY DOCTOR!

Annnnnd done.

Greyson got two stitches in his chin that night and only shed a single tear. Never change, Danger Baby. Except maybe stop doing handstands on bathtubs.

DON'T DO THAT is an incentive.

I TOLD YOU SO is vindication.

Dan's DADVICE

2008 - 2012

chapter

21

the Rainbow Baby

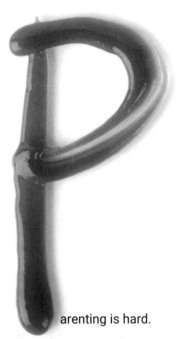arenting is hard.

But making a baby, that's easy, right? It sure sounds easy. And fun. Do the deed, get a baby. It seems like everyone I know had it happen like that. They did the hokey-pokey, made some peanut-butter-jelly-time, studied human anatomy, got a "backrub," whatever'd the humdinger and viola—nine months later they got a baby.

It doesn't always work like that.

Making a baby can be heartbreaking, and unless you've experienced that specific kind of heartbreak it's hard to understand or relate to it. I sat down many times to put this chapter together but the words never felt right. They always felt sad or boring. Sometimes both. The tone of this book is supposed to be humorous. It's not a serious book. I'm not a serious person. I continuously asked myself, how can I make this funny? Does this chapter have to be funny?

I decided it didn't have to be funny. It should be honest. And while this is a hard chapter to write it may very well be the most important one because it all started here. Literally everything started here—this book, the stories, the adventures in raising three boys, our family, our lives.

Everything happens for a reason. For the record, I'm often reluctant to agree with that notion but it's undeniable. Shit happens. Call it what you want—destiny, happenstance or luck. No matter how hard you try you cannot control it. You can only control your reaction.

Crystal and I really, really wanted to be parents. We were trying. We read books, blogs, attended classes and talked about the names and lives of our future children. I swore my firstborn son would be named Barracuda Johnson. That name sounded so badass! Like an MMA fighter or a cyborg.

President Barracuda Johnson on the other hand, sounded ridiculous. Damn it. That's a cool name but would that cool name limit the career choices of my firstborn later in life? Probably. We're not celebrities, we couldn't give our kids names like Pomegranate or Barracuda Johnson. Those names would stick out on resumes, business cards, mortgage applications, etc. We had to find something more...conventional. But not too vanilla. So we kept talking and we kept dreaming.

The next conversation, for a lot of people, is OMFG we're pregnant! How should we tell everyone?! What kind of gender reveal should we have?! Let's start a hashtag! Cupcakes or cake?! What about cake pops? Everyone loves cake pops!

For most parents-to-be, their worries starts the minute that pee test turns blue. Will baby girl or baby boy be healthy? Will Mom be healthy? Will baby girl or baby boy stay healthy? Will Mom stay healthy? Will I be a good parent? Will baby girl or baby boy like me? They have to, right? What's a mucus plug? I saw a vaginal delivery video in tenth grade biology class. I'm gonna pass out. Thanks, Mr. Marsh.

We weren't those people.

Our worries started earlier. We had a hard time. We faced challenges the books didn't prepare us for. We lost a child, Gavin Max, during the third trimester. Fuck you, trisomy two.

That hurt. It still hurts. But Crystal and I grew closer and matured. We struggled. We cried. We tried. We cried some more. We kept trying. And trying. And crying. We faced surgeries, together. Testing, together. Fertility treatments, together. More heartache, together. More tears. More bullshit that other people couldn't understand.

We faced stupid questions from people. "When are you guys going to have kids?" they'd ask, or "We thought you'd have kids by now." The worst was, "I heard you guys were pregnant. Where's the baby? Are you sure you don't have a baby?"

"Yeah fuck face, we're sure we don't have a baby. Do you mind if we finish grocery shopping now?"

Those questions only break spirits more than they're already broken. They sink into every fiber of your being and make you wonder what's wrong with you. Are you broken? Why isn't your body doing what it should be doing? We're good people, right? Shouldn't good things happen to good people? We began to experience a new emotion, together. Sadness meets boiling anger.

For the record, don't ask anyone those questions. Ever. It's none of your concern.

We kept trying, for years, because we really, really wanted to be parents. Eventually, trying became a chore. It had to be calculated around shots and peak ovulation periods.

After a while we decided to cool it for a bit. We wanted to focus on us. We needed a change, so we bought a house and brought home a bulldog puppy named Penelope. She would be our fur baby since the furless kind wasn't happening.

Then it happened. The pee test turned blue.

WTF? It just happened. Like it just happens to everyone else. We couldn't believe it. New house. New puppy. A new light at the end of a new tunnel. We weren't even unpacked yet! Ok, Crystal was. I wasn't.

The worrying started again. We were high-risk this time around. It felt like there was a doctor's appointment every week. The entire pregnancy was filled with stress and endless worries.

But the baby was healthy and growing and doing all those fetal things he or she should be doing every week, like measuring the size of a poppy seed, peppercorn, pomegranate seed, blueberry, raspberry, cherry, kumquat, fig, plum.

In case you're wondering, the plum size is where fingernails, toenails and little itty bitty baby bones start forming. No wonder pregnancy cravings are a thing, fetal progress is measured in food.

Even with the constant reassurance of our doctors, we still had that unrelenting nagging voice in the backs of heads whispering worries and what-ifs. We tried our best to ignore it. Somewhere between sweet potato and banana we found out the baby was a boy, and while I still loved the name Barracuda Johnson we thought Paxton Max was a more conventional, but not too vanilla, fit.

Crystal and Paxton Max were doing good. The pregnancy seemed like it was pretty normal. Nothing too stressful, just lots and lots of doctors appointments filled with lots and lots of reassuring conversations with our doctors that Paxton was growing and healthy.

Week thirty-seven rolled around and the doctors noticed a change in Crystal. She was developing (or had developed) preeclampsia. Our doctors scheduled an emergency induction.

We left their office and drove straight to the hospital. For me that was a bit unexpected. For Crystal? Not so much. She's super organized in every aspect of life so her and Pax's hospital bags were already in the car. Her motherly intuition was already in full swing.

Paxton Max came into this world on July 6th, 2012 at 6:03 PM after a brief thirty-six hour labor. Our journey into parenthood was only beginning.

I cut the cord and made my first official Dad Joke. "Gee, this would be easier to cut if I brought my giant ceremonial scissors."

I laughed. No one else did.

Crystal was too weak from the magnesium and pitocin cocktail to lift her arms. She couldn't hold Paxton, so the nurses swaddled him and laid him on her chest. We shared a very brief moment as a family of three before Paxton was whisked off to the NICU.

I thought Crystal was going to die during delivery at one point. The magnesium was brutal. I can't really explain what happened other than it didn't seem normal. She was lethargic, quiet, pale. Like she was falling asleep or passing out. The doctors saw this too and took her off it. She was able to somehow power through the last few contractions and pushed Paxton out.

I later asked her what got her through those moments.

"Gavin," she responded.

Thanks for the help, little man.

Initially we were told Paxton was going to the NICU as a precaution since he was in the birth canal for a long time. He also had a large hematoma on his umbilical cord that needed examined. Our doctors were concerned his intestines had been strained and may have been pulled through his belly button into the umbilical cord during labor.

They told us they'd clean him up, examine him and bring him back to us in a couple of hours. Those couple of hours turned into seven days.

The hematoma was nothing more than a big ol' bruise which was a relief, but his white blood count was incredibly low. So low that the

NICU staff thought it was an error. There were talks of a transfusion if the levels didn't begin to rise independently.

In the meantime, the doctors turned their attention to Crystal. Her preeclampsia became postpartum preeclampsia which kept her bound to her bed while our newborn son was in the NICU on the other side of the hospital.

She couldn't leave her room to visit, hold, feed or change him and he couldn't leave the NICU. For the first five days of Paxton's life Mom could only see him through pictures and videos I took while visiting, feeding and changing him.

I took a lot of photos and videos. They were the only way Crystal could see Paxton. I held his hands, told him stories, talked about his Mom, watched him sleep and fed him. I opted to not hold him yet. I wanted Crystal to be the first person to hold him. She deserved that honor more than anyone.

On the fifth day, Crystal was finally cleared to leave her room and she got to hold Paxton for the first time. Some serious Momma snuggles ensued.

Crystal was discharged one day later but we didn't leave the hospital until much, much later that night. We spent hours with Pax in the NICU. He was doing great, getting stronger, less jaundice-y and his white blood count course corrected itself independently. And he was crapping up a storm.

Newborn poop is weird. Have fun with that if you haven't already experienced it.

On July 12th, Paxton Max came home from the hospital. Hell yeah! Crystal's motherly intuition was right, again. She had Paxton's coming-home outfit ready to go. His bags were packed and in the car before the sun came up that morning. She had a feeling he'd be coming home that day.

Every year we celebrate the 6th and the 12th with Pax. The 6th is, of course, the big birthday hoopla. The 12th is a smaller hoopla that reminds us to be thankful for our family and our health.

The whole experience of wanting and waiting to become parents taught us a lot about what it actually meant to be a parent.

First, your situation is only as bad as you make it. Yes, it was a struggle but Crystal and I always made time for one another. We're a team and a good team supports each other. We shared laughs, even on those really bad days, and kept smiling the best we could as we reminded ourselves that things could be worse.

We realize our journey into parenthood was different than a lot of other parents. We faced some difficult moments. But we faced everything together. It made us stronger as a couple, as individuals, and as parents.

We learned parents have to be patient. But remember to parent. It's ok to get upset, to get mad and yell. Correct your kids when they need to understand something bigger than themselves and their actions. I get mad. I yell. I correct my kids. Pick your battles. Remember they're kids and they need room to grow and find themselves. Give them space but keep them close so they feel comfortable enough to talk to you about anything.

Parents also have to be optimistic. Find the good in the bad and use that as learning experience. So your kid just yelled, "SON OF A BITCH NEW PAW PATROL!" in Target or they brought home a blue slip for "being Billy Madison during quiet time." Talk to them about it and find the good in those situations. Even if "the good" is laughing with your significant other about the ordeal after the kids are in bed.

Being a parent is hard but it gets easier.

Eventually.

END every day with a LAUGH.

Dan's DADVICE

2014

chapter

22

hose first kid vs. second kid diaper commercials are pretty accurate. You'll relax and learn a thing or two about being a parent when you have multiple kids.

For instance, oversized diaper bags are a waste of money. Gimme a trendy gender-neutral backpack that looks sexy on both Mom and Dad while expertly holding diapers, wipes, snacks and toys because we can't live without those things.

Did you just feed your baby and he or she spit up? Did some of it land in or around your mouth? Big deal! Today is laundry day, wipe it on your shirt! Technically every day is laundry day, but who's keeping track?

You'll only need two wipes to clean a poopy diaper. Two! Even for those mustard pump poops that grossed you out back in the day. Your chump days are behind you, Hoss.

What the diaper commercials do not tell you is that the reason you become more lax as a parent is because going from one to two children is utterly insane. There is no time to overprepare, no time to care what your diaper bag looks like. Especially when your now brood of two is only twenty months apart and still in diapers.

Crystal and I found out that Paxton was going to be a big brother a day or so before his first birthday. A forever friend? What a great gift! Paxton was still a little guy but he understood what we told him and was excited for a "bay bee."

But having been through this twice before, our same old worries started up the minute that pee test turned blue. Will baby girl or baby boy be healthy? Will Mom be healthy? Will baby girl or baby boy stay healthy? Will Mom be healthy this time?

On top of all that, a fresh crop of new concerns we'd never anticipated took root. I'm a good parent with one how will I handle two? Will baby girl or baby boy like me as much as Paxton likes me? Will he or she have their mornings and nights mixed up? Will the kids get along? I got along with my siblings, I think? I know what a mucus plug is now, so that's cool. I saw a vaginal delivery in real life and I did not pass out. Sophomore me would be impressed.

Things sure were different this time around. The pregnancy was easy, at least from my vantage point. Mom and baby were healthy from the beginning and stayed that way for the entire pregnancy. The sweet potato/banana milestone hit and we found out this baby had a penis too! We were going to have another boy! I could only imagine what kind of mischief big brother and little brother would get into. I couldn't wait to encourage it.

Let's jump ahead to thirty-eight weeks plus two days. Our doctors scheduled an induction. Nothing out of the ordinary, just time to have the baby. The delivery this time was faster. Admitted at 5:00 AM. Pitocin started at 6:00 AM. Colton Broox made his debut at 3:01 PM on March 5th, 2014.

It was a new record! Out within thirty-six hours! Mom did great. Mom looks great. Mom is great. She's a pro. High fives all the way around the delivery room. I stepped over to the scale and greeted my son for the first time.

ME: Ohhh Paxton, you are so cute.

I lift my camera to take a photo.

CRYSTAL: DAN!

I jump. I quickly turn around. I see my lovely wife, feet elevated, getting stitched up. Her eyes are burning holes into me.

ME: What?

"THAT'S COLTON!!!"

I look at my son. He looks at me.

ME: FAAAAAAAAAAAAAACK! COLTON! I AM SO SORRY. I knew this would happen but didn't think it would happen this fast. Thirty seconds old and I already called you the wrong name. Oh my God. I am so sorry. Let me try this again...Ohhh COLTON, you are so cute.

I'm 100% positive this is the reason Colton hates the word cute. HATES it. It's my fault. Not even a minute into life and I greeted him by the wrong name.

From day one I'm convinced he learned to associate "cute" with absent mindedness—something else that he isn't too fond of.

You're probably thinking he was thirty seconds old don't be so hard on yourself. You shush your face. I saw the look he gave me. It was the look of betrayal.

Colton is like a little elephant. He does not forget. Seriously. I left my wallet at Dunkin' Donuts once. Now every time he sees a donut, we pass a Dunkin', or a commercial airs on TV he looks at me and asks the same question.

"Remember that time when you took us to Dunkin' Donuts then we went to Target and in the checkout you remembered you left your wallet at Dunkin' Donuts so we had to leave everything and go back to Dunkin' to get your wallet and then back to Target and you said don't tell Mom?"

"Dude. That was like five years ago, but yes I still remember because you won't let me forget."

I know he heard and understood what I said in the delivery room. Not only did I call him the wrong name. I called him the "C" word.

I am so sorry for calling you cute, Colton. I'm sorry I ruined that word for you at such a young age.

I'm also sorry for calling you Paxton within the first minute of your life. I will never forgive myself for that.

If Colton could have chopped my head off, I know he would have.

Sorry about the
Pennsylvania Dutch Oven.
Six taco dinner!

♡ A HAIKU FROM HUSBAND TO WIFE ♡

2016

chapter
23

You experience a whirlwind of emotions as a parent. It comes with the territory and everyday is different. Being a dad is non-stop. Being a mom is ten times as demanding.

Despite all the countless moments and crazy memories, one day in particular will always stand out to me. It was the first day that I ever felt truly surprised. Genuinely shocked. Pure unadulterated excitement. I'm fairly certain Crystal felt those same feelings on January 13, 2016.

I was in the midst of some crazy new business pitch at work. Stressed the fuck out because deadlines weren't changing but the deliverables were. That's life in advertising, right? I guess so. It sucks but it's business.

I just got out of some bullshit meeting that involved a lot of talking in circles. As I stepped out of the conference room I felt the *bzzt *bzzt of a text message in my pocket.

I stopped walking, reached for my phone and looked at the screen.

The thumbnail showed Paxton and Colton dressed in matching shirts. They were smiling and holding something. I opened the message.

Holy. Fucking. Shit.

It's a pee test.

And it's blue.

IT'S BLUE?!

My mood instantly shifted. Everything that happened before this message was white noise. That shit didn't matter. This did.

I was speechless. I stood outside of the conference room with my jaw wide open. I could feel tears in my eyes.

This feeling is exactly how Greyson greets us every morning. He smiles so hard that his cheeks look like they're porcelain. It's infectious. He loves sneaking up on Crystal and me with that smile just like he did on January 13, 2016. Then he kicks me in the shin and runs away. G completes our family—like the cheese on top of a chili dog. Sure, it's good without cheese but *with* cheese it's perfect.

The next forty weeks were a healthy blur.

For the first time we were experiencing a normal pregnancy. Technically, Colton was a normal pregnancy but we still worried constantly. This was the first one free from worry. We just enjoyed it. The boys enjoyed it. Our family was almost complete.

We had our one and only gender reveal party. Crystal and I knew this would be our last baby so we decided to do all the stupid trendy stuff that everyone else does. Paxton and I were on team girl. Crystal was on team boy. Colton was on team M&M's. I tried to explain that M&M's were candy-coated chocolate and not a gender, but he just chopped my head off and then ate his weight in cake pops.

My sister picked up cans of gender-specific silly string. A group of our closest friends and family counted down in the backyard. They aimed the nozzles at the four of us.

Deep down Crystal and I knew what was coming.

A wave of blue covered us. Colton panicked. He hates silly string. It's far too silly for him.

A third boy.

Oh boy.

Let's do this.

Week forty rolled around and we headed to the hospital for induction. Crystal settled into her delivery suite and got hooked up to the usual contraptions. She dilated fast, four centimeters. Geez, we just got here. Muscle memory must be a real thing. It was now or never for the epidural so I stepped out to grab a salad at the hospital cafeteria while she got stabbed in the back.

I had hours until the little man made his debut, right?

I ate my salad and went back to Crystal's room. I walked in and saw my wife resting. I decided to do the same and sat on the chair next to her bed.

POP

She sat up. "I think that was my water."

"Damn. That was loud," I said. "Sounded like a balloon popping."

Suddenly her monitors went crazy. Greyson's heart rate began to drop. The doctors rushed in and checked stuff out. They reassured us that everything was ok but they looked serious, concerned almost.

"10 centimeters. Time to push."

She dilated six centimeters in the time it took me to eat a salad? Impressive.

Four minutes later Greyson was out. A new record! Knowing Greyson now I'm not surprised his delivery was so fast. He's a fast kid. Why should his birth be any different?

Fuck.

He's blue.

Really blue.

Why is he so blue?

The room is quiet.

Why is the room so quiet?

Crystal takes a breath. "Dan, Why isn't he crying?"

The silence in the room was broken by Greyson's first cry. The blue faded from his face and body. He opened his eyes and looked at Crystal for the first time.

I leaned in to cut the cord, holding back my ceremonial scissor Dad Jokes. Not because I didn't want to make them but because I saw why he wasn't crying.

His umbilical cord was tied in a knot. A very tight knot. A knot that would have resulted in a very different outcome had he stayed in the womb any longer.

Four minutes.

Those minutes felt like a blink. That was dangerous, right? It was. The doctor's remarks confirmed my almost fears.

"Good thing he came out when he did," she said as she held up the tangled cord.

That's Greyson Knox in a nutshell. He's fast. He's dangerous. And on September 6, 2016 at 12:12 PM, he made an entrance that was equal parts both.

★ before ★
__Baby's first haircut__

★ after ★
Baby's first haircut

chapter
24

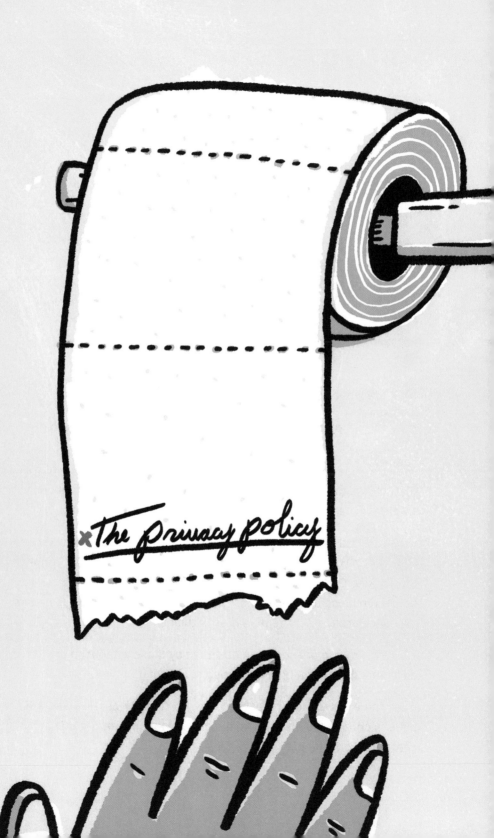

any moons ago I could use the bathroom without interruption. Now I'm lucky if I can get the door closed before there's a little knock knock knock from the other side.

"Daaaaad, I have to pee like really, really, really, really bad."

"Well, I'm pooping. You need to go use the downstairs bathroom."

"I can't. I have to pee too bad to walk down the steps."

This is the epitome of parenting. Getting off the toilet mid-poop so your kid can use the bathroom.

I started asking the boys if they had to use the bathroom before I do. They always say no. I double check. Still no. Triple check. Nope! Stop asking Dad, we don't need to pee or poop. Then as I relax and let nature run its course, the same little knock knock knock always breaks my concentration. This routine is as regular as I am.

Privacy is a phenomenon observed by those without young children. I don't like it but I've learned to accept it.

There will come a time when they won't knock on the door. Until then, I'll continue to stealthily make my way to the bathroom. That seems to work one out of ten times.

Bathrooms fascinate my kids. They love bathrooms.

It's weird but cool, I guess. They get to see a lot of bathrooms since I travel for work a good bit. When I'm on the road I FaceTime with the family a few times a day. Without fail, the boys are always more interested in what the bathroom looks like in my hotel room over anything I say. They don't care about impeccable tile work or the intricate details interior designers put into these boutique hotels. I love those things but my kids just want to see where Dad's gonna poop for the week since they won't be there to jam their little fingers under the bathroom door. Bathrooms give us something to talk about as the three of them fight over who can squeeze their face closest to the camera.

At least they're consistent.

Paxton especially loves bathrooms. The kid pees a lot. He also drinks a lot of water. We've had conversations with his teachers and doctors about it. Nothing is wrong. He just always has to go and always goes when he says he has to. Even if he just went before we left the house.

Every time we go somewhere new he has to go to the bathroom. Someone's house, a restaurant, a store, rest stop, etc. He'll always ask if the place has a bathroom.

When we tell him no, he responds, "But I have to pee like really, really, really, really bad," just loud enough so the employee hears.

"Sorry buddy. No public bathroom. Store policy."

We think part of it is that Paxton just really likes to see what bathrooms look like. If you think about it, bathrooms are always different. They're like snowflakes or fingerprints, no two are identical.

The bathroom thing follows us everywhere. 50% curiosity and 50% emergency. The latter half is the reason parking lot potty breaks became a thing for a while.

I'm not proud to admit that.

For those of you wondering, a parking lot potty break is exactly what it sounds like. Peeing in a parking lot. More specifically a kid or kids peeing on our car tire in a parking lot.

I know public urination is frowned upon but when a kid's gotta go, a kid's gonna go. Thankfully, parking lot potty breaks are becoming far less frequent with the older boys and G hasn't started potty training yet so he most likely won't pee on tires like his big brothers did, since third kids follow the lead of the older ones. If he doesn't see them peeing on cars then he won't pee on cars. Problem solved. I hope.

Parking lot potty breaks were more of a potty training thing anyway. A little bladder can only hold pee for so long before pants get ruined and feelings get hurt. Peeing on a tire sometimes is the best option because kids at that age tell you they have to pee the moment the levee is about to break. Believe it or not parking lot potty breaks actually aid in potty training.

When boys potty train it's a great idea to talk to them about their aim from day one. Aiming requires finesse. Finesse comes with practice. That's why we decided to †start potty training outside.

We figured our backyard was the perfect training ground. A wide open space to practice and make mistakes and learn from those mistakes. With any luck they'd be the Steve Nashes of the bathroom and set records-shattering pee throws.

It was working. Colton and Paxton learned what the pre-pee feeling felt like and would stop playing to go. Mom carried hand sanitizer around with her at all times, so they'd run over to tell us they peed and would get a squirt of sanitizer then a high five before returning to play.

Soon they could hit a big target like a tree or fence from fifteen feet away with a hell of an arc. Great. Let's try ten feet. Awesome. Five feet. Stupendous. One foot. BINGO!

It was soon time to practice accuracy inside.

But the transition from backyard to bathroom didn't go as planned. The boys would ignore the toilet and instead open the back door, walk outside to a tree and pee on it.

Crap. That backfired. I couldn't have the weird kids who only pee outside.

I sat Paxton and Colton down and explained that when we are inside we use the bathroom and wash our hands. They understood and started peeing in the bathroom like civilized creatures. That was an easy conversation followed by an easy win.

Their aim however, never reached backyard accuracy again.

Boys have terrible aim. Even when you think everything is lined up there are those moments you misfire. Just because an eyeball and a penis are facing the same direction doesn't mean they're looking at the same thing.

Sometimes you miss by a little. Sometimes you miss by a lot. A miss is a miss. We worked on our aim together. We had to. I was tired of stepping in puddles of pee everytime I walked into the bathroom.

One day I brought both boys into the bathroom and had them clean up their pee puddles. They knew which one was theirs which meant they knew they missed and decided to just leave it alone. Lovely. I had to show them how this was done.

I demonstrated proper aim. You stand nice and close to the toilet, you look where you want to pee, gently point your weiner downward, lean forward a bit if you need to and go.

DAMN IT!

I missed the toilet. I freaking rimmed it and hit the floor.

The boys thought that was hilarious. There I was, lecturing them on how to aim and I did exactly what I told them not to do. Dad's a schmuck.

I cleaned up my puddle, washed my hands and ran to the kitchen. I returned with a handful of Goldfish crackers.

"Here, shoot at these," I said, tossing tiny crackers into the toilet.

But wait? Why not sit to pee? I had that conversation. They wanted to be like Dad and stand up. When your kids tell you they want to be like you, that's the highest honor a parent can receive, next to getting your head chopped off.

So, I taught them to stand. I bought them a small blue foot stool to stand on since they neither one of them were tall enough to get their dinker over the edge of the toilet.

Paxton outgrew the stool before Colton. Colton did not like that Paxton, his older brother, was a few inches taller. He thought Paxton had an unfair and unjustified height advantage, and hey, he was a big brother just like Paxton now, so he did not want to use the stool anymore. But he had to. He was aiming up and peeing over the toilet.

Using the foot stool became a battle. Colton decided when he would stop wearing diapers and now he decided he wasn't going to use that footstool. Wonderful.

One evening as Crystal and I prepared dinner, I heard fits of laughter coming from the bathroom.

GREYSON: OH NO RUN!!!!

Greyson runs down the hall, jumps on the couch and hides behind the cushions.

Uproarious laughter echoes throughout our home.

PAXTON: Woah. Woah. AHHH!

COLTON: Oh man!

Uproarious laughter continues.

PAXTON: Colton! ColTON! COLTON!

This doesn't sound good.

COLTON:: WATCH OUT!

PAXTON: Woah. HA HA!

Greyson runs back down the hallway toward the bathroom. He stops at the door. He screams.

GREYSON: AHHHHHHHHHH PEE PEE!!!!!

PAXTON: Ah! You almost got me.

COLTON: Stop! I'm trying! I'm really trying!

Ok. I need to see what's happening now. I step into the hallway.

The scene unfolded in slow motion like an action movie minus the explosions. Greyson turned away with a look of fear in his eyes. He ducked under my legs and ran screaming to the living room, his long blonde hair blowing back. He clutched a bag of Goldfish crackers in his hands. Goldfish fell to the floor as he ran, crumbling on impact.

I looked up. The bathroom door slid open. Paxton fell backward through the doorway and into the hall. His pants and underwear were around his ankles. He was still peeing.

His face was red with laughter, his mouth and eyes wide open. He hit the floor as his feet continued moving up and over his head. Still peeing.

Paxton slid across the hallway. He attempted to stop the pee by covering his weiner with his hands. Ever try to stop a garden hose like that? The water doesn't stop. It just sprays faster and in every direction. Yup. Penises work a lot like garden hoses.

I decided not to deal with that right away. I had to see if something more devastating was waiting for me in the bathroom.

I stepped over Paxton and around Greyson's trail of goldfish, crushing several under my feet. I didn't care. I was on a mission.

In the bathroom I saw Colton. His pants and underwear were also around his ankles. He looked worried.

He was standing close to the toilet, like I said to do. He was leaning forward, like I said to do. He was gently pointing his weiner down, like I said to do.

But, he was on his tippy toes. He was struggling to maintain balance as his socks caused his feet to slide backward on the tile floor. Still peeing, he was trying to "walk" toward the toilet but he was unable to stay upright.

Pee was ricocheting off the rim of the toilet, spraying up, spraying down, spraying sideways, to the left, to the right, everywhere as his socks continued to move him away from the toilet.

Finally, Colton stopped peeing.

He relaxed and stood flat-footed. He wasn't laughing anymore. My son looked scared and exhausted, like he'd just panicked for the first time in his life. He looked me dead in the eye and exhaled.

"I'm not tall enough."

ME: No big deal, dude. It's just pee.

COLTON: Sorry.

ME: You tried and that's all that matters, right?

COLTON: Right. I love you, Dad.

ME: I love you, too.

Colton was so disappointed in himself. Poor guy. He thought I was going to be mad. How could I be? I've peed all over the bathroom before, even as an adult.

Life would be much simpler if we could just pee on trees.

†Legally I need to advise against peeing outside. Yes, it works. Yes, it's fun. Yes, technically speaking you can do it. Should you? I don't know. Probably not. You're an adult, make your own choices. If you pee outside be smart about where and when you do it. I tell my boys you can pee outside if you do so behind a tree in your own backyard while no one is looking. Don't pee on buildings or someone else's car tire and never pee in your neighbor's yard.

259

Buy the Flushable WiPes!

Your butthole is worth it too. One final pass with a wipe keeps the wrinkle biscuit feeling fresh.

DaN's DADVICE

2016

chapter

25

Three years ago I decided to start writing these stories down. It was a Friday afternoon. I was sitting on my couch with a bag of frozen peas on my lap and an Xbox controller in my hand. Crystal (who was pregnant with Greyson at the time) took Paxton and Colton to Grammy and Pap-Pap's for a weekend sleepover. Our house was hushed with a calm I hadn't experienced since our pre-kid days.

I had a vasectomy that morning and was home alone with my video games and my thoughts. The slight stinging from the incision made me think about my earlier emergency room predicament. I started laughing to myself about how bizarre that entire ordeal was. The pain. The ultrasound. The encounter at Target a few days later.

That memory lead to another which lead to another and another. I sat on the couch with the Jolly Green Giant on my lap and a stupid smile on my face.

The house was quiet and lonely. It's always like that when the kids aren't home. It's weird. Their constant noise can be obnoxious. But when that noise is gone you realize how boring life is without kids. The noise becomes a comfort.

I missed them but I was thankful that I could relax without fear of getting hit in the goods for forty-eight hours. It was a weekday and when Dad is home on a weekday the boys get super-duper excited. Super-duper excited boys lead to super-duper injuries like infections, sliced eyeballs, busted up chins, etc.

When Crystal tells someone that we have three boys she gets some variation of the same response—"Oh honey. Three boys. Bless you." Yes, we are #blessed. Our dudes are amazing. Sure they're crazy. And loud. And annoying at times. They prevent Crystal and I from carrying on an uninterrupted conversation. They've chipped my teeth and hospitalized me. They've peed on the bathroom floor, our cars, trees, me, each other, and God knows what else. They make fart jokes. They make weiner jokes. They make up jokes that make no sense. They break things. They ask an overwhelmingly high number of questions and they don't listen to the overwhelmingly high number of answers. But we wouldn't have it any other way.

Greyson, Colton and Paxton are three creative, energetic, and happy boys. They're filled with curiosity and a willingness to try new things unless those new things are carrots, broccoli or any food outside of our five basic food groups. But, that's fine by me. Our house is filled with hot dogs and love.

Or, as Colton puts it...

" Our house may be small but the laughs in it are big."

Despite all his antics he is actually a very sweet and caring boy. If he heard me say that then he'd make angry face, growl and cut my head off. That's just his hard exterior masking his soft squishy doughy center.

Paxton always talks about his life when he grows up and every little detail mirrors the life he has now but he's older and drives a concrete mixer. He lives in a little house with a red roof, a big yard and marries a sweet girl. They have three sons together.

Danger Baby is still very dangerous but now he's a little more affectionate. He stopped biting and started kissing. Greyson will always be a combo of Dennis the Menace and Taz. Since I started writing this book he's added a pinch of The Incredible Hulk and a dash of Bill Watterson's Calvin to his personality mix. I look forward to watching his personality blossom.

I also look forward to karma coming back to visit me when the three of them are teenagers. I know what I did as a teenager. My parents, on the other hand, only know the things that I was caught doing. Karma's coming back in threes.

Kids are only kids for a very brief period of time, so live it up and have fun alongside of them. Celebrate the crazy and encourage it. The crazy makes memories. We learn as much from them as they learn from us. Kids teach you patience. They help you slow down and appreciate the little things.

Greyson loves to stop and smell the flowers. Literally. He stops at every flower he sees and makes time to appreciate their smells and their colors like EYE EYE, HULK and purple. That mentality is something we've worked really hard to instill in our boys. It's a great feeling seeing them live by the examples Crystal and I set.

We have fun with our kids. We love being parents. We're working our asses off to raise three gentlemen but life is too short to be strict and boring. We jump on the couch, build forts and cuddle. We swear, have food fights and practice table manners. We listen to Dead Kennedys, have mosh pits in our living room and say "please" and "thank you." Becoming a parent taught Crystal and I a lot of things but most importantly it taught us to not get hung up on the little things. Kids are kids. They learn by example. Be that example.

Unless you're an asshole.

If you are an asshole then there's a strong possibility that your kid is going to be an asshole, too. Don't raise assholes. The world needs less assholes and more kindness and understanding.

It's not easy and it's not supposed to be. Parenthood is a non-stop tiresome adventure. There are good days, bad days and so-so days. Regardless of what kind of day it was, we tell the boys the same things every night before bed.

"I love you."

"I'm proud of you."

"I'm so happy to have you in my life."

They say the same thing.

We turn off the lights and close their doors.

Then we hear,

And bedtime drags on for another thirteen minutes.

M-O-M spells Mom.
You are everything to us!
Family Keystone.

♡ A HAIKU FROM HUSBAND TO WIFE ♡

Acknowledgments

This book is like a baby. It took time and effort to make and push it out into the world. But it wouldn't be possible without some help from some great people like...

My boys, duh. I did this for the three of you. I wanted you to have something unique when you're older. This way when you call me in twenty-five years and tell me you're sorry for punching me in the nuts I can just tell you to read the book and write your own. So, thank you Greyson, Colton and Paxton. Thank you for the stories, the laughs and for making me a better dad. Always be yourself.

Crystal!!! My BFF and partner in crime all these years. You're a rockstar Mom/Wife/Human and without you and your uterus none of this would be possible. Seriously. The world needs more people like you. You're patient, loving, kind and I admire everything about you. I love you.

Animal Media Group, Howard Shapiro and Michael Killen. You provided me with the opportunity to turn my notes and doodles into a book. Not many professional conversations start with, "I had this infection."

Alaina Sapienza. Your reading and revising and reading and revising and reading and revising was incredibly helpful in bringing *Hot Dog People* to life. Now you know the difference between "weiners" and "wieners!"

My folks, Theresa and George Magdich. Thanks Mom and Dad for doing the deed in 1986 and for raising me in a household where my creativity was encouraged. Even if I drew some really weird shit like aliens eating people and "cannons" that were totally not cannons. They were definitely penises, Mom.

My in-laws, Melinda and Bob O'Brien. Without you two there would be no Crystal. So thank you for also doing the deed and raising an incredible daughter. I'll drink to that!

Doug Helmick and PLASMID. You guys wrote and recorded an album of *Hot Dog People* inspired songs. I love you sweaty punk rockers so much for that. The living room mosh pit is now dedicated to you.

David Kelly. Thank you for shooting the cover and the "I HATE KETCHUP" font. Your studio smelled terrible but the shots gave this book the extra pizzazz I wanted.

Frank Vilsack. Thank you for the family photos and for your willingness to stand in the ketchup, mustard and hot dog crossfire.

YOU. Yeah you, the one holding this book right now! Thank you for purchasing (or stealing) *Hot Dog People*. Hopefully you bought it because book sales help fill the Snack Box. I hope you enjoyed reading it regardless of how you obtained this copy.

Old Man Joesa. I don't know who you were or how you're connected to Colton but thank you. I'm sorry you got shot in the eye and died. Give my best to Lacey.

Hot Dog People and Other Bite-Size Sacrifices is complete, for now. The stories will continue. They will get crazier, involve more injuries and more things said at inappropriate times. So maybe there will be a second volume? I can only imagine what the puberty years have in store for us.

Thanks for reading.
- Dan

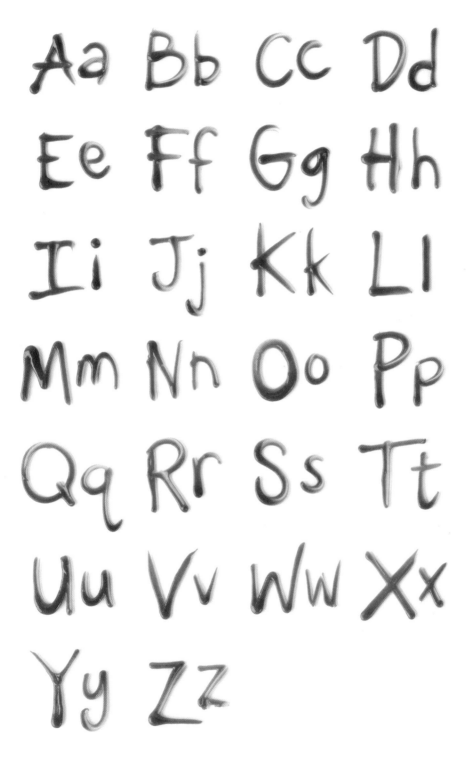